AF504139

To David –

A soleil 3? A tentative 2?
Surely not a 1!!!

Cheers,

[signature]

2004

Once A Dancer

by

Patrick McIntyre

The Memoir Club

First published in 2003 by
The Memoir Club
Whitworth Hall
Spennymoor
County Durham

British Library Cataloguing in
Publication Data.
A catalogue record for this book
is available from the
British Library.

ISBN: 1 84104 081 9

Typeset by George Wishart & Associates, Whitley Bay.
Printed by CPI Bath

In memory of dear Peg

Contents

Illustrations

Acknowledgements

THE IDEA OF writing a book about my life had never occurred to me until friends and dinner party companions began nagging me to get my anecdotes down on paper. In a career as long as mine one self-censors reminiscences to avoid the 'boring old theatrical fart' tag, but people appeared to find what seemed everyday occurrences to me interesting and extraordinary. Many thanks therefore to all who nagged. It's all your fault!

I'd like to thank Anne Marriott who typed my early chapters at break-neck speed from my Dictaphone tapes until I gathered the courage to write straight onto the computer, and a special thank you to my cousin Linda who is the custodian of the Gair Bible for her help in untangling the family tree.

Finally there are two men on either side of the Atlantic whose boundless enthusiasm for the project kept me focussed and determined; Percy Saltzman in Canada and Mark Woolgar here in the UK. Gentlemen, I salute you.

Chapter One

Made in Manhattan, reared on the prairies…a dancing extra-terrestrial…forefathers, plucky pioneers and/or black sheep…fateful decision aged eight…first performance aged ten

MAYBE IT WAS the drama of the underdogs, Detroit, winning the pennant that year or perhaps just the excitement of being in the Big Apple for the first time, but my parents, while attending the 1935 Baseball World Series in New York got – as family legend puts it – 'frisky'. In consequence, the following summer back home in Winnipeg, known as the Gateway to the West on the Canadian prairies, I arrived as the latest member of the McIntyre clan, very unexpectedly and totally unplanned.

My parents had finished their family, as they thought, six years earlier with the arrival of my brother, Owen. They already had a daughter, Marguerite, and when Owen came along that was that. Besides, my mother was minus a kidney. She'd had it removed some years earlier and, in the 1930s, this was a risky procedure. Although she lived a long and vigorous life surviving on only one, it was certainly considered dangerous to embark on another pregnancy. However, all went well, apart from the fact that I arrived in the middle of a heat wave. The temperature hovered over or just under 100°F for the three weeks before I was born on 18 June 1936.

Although I seemed a bonny and cheerful child, (I won second prize in a Beautiful Baby competition!) what they couldn't know then, of course, was that I had been dropped from another planet. I had nothing in common with the other children around me or indeed with my family. It was as if I was a dancing ET. I had a blissfully happy early childhood, totally unaware of how odd I must have seemed to the rest of the world. I thought it was perfectly ordinary for a child to jump and skip and hop and twirl down the main street of the town after seeing a matinée of a Gene Kelly movie and thought it strange that everyone

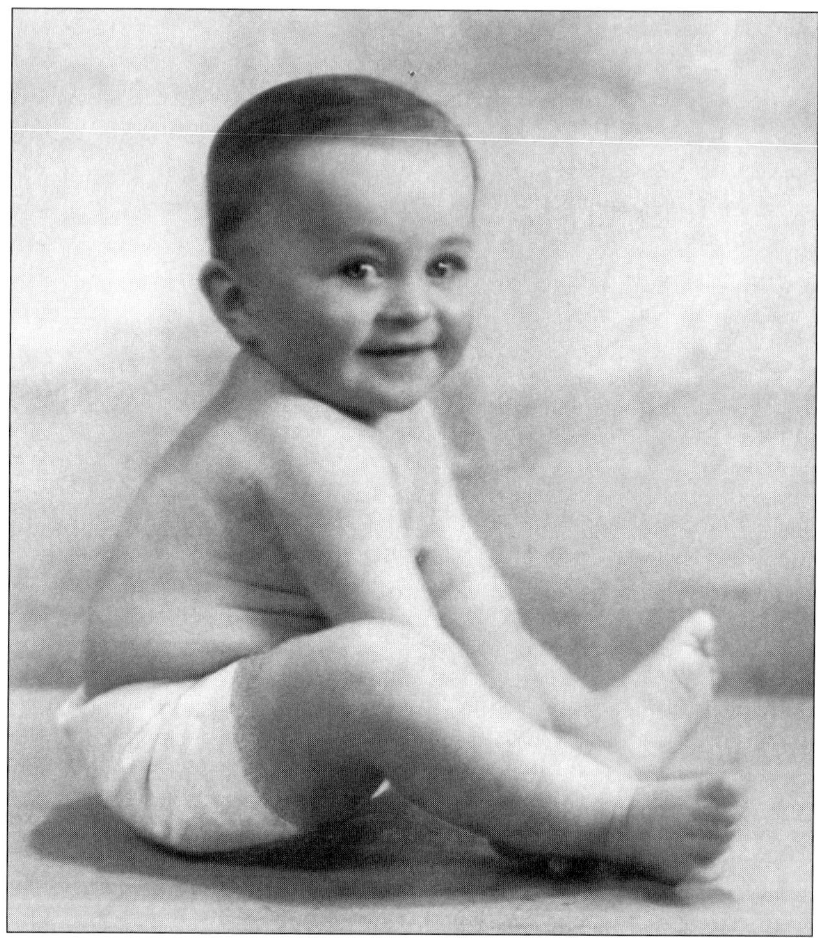

What do you mean 2nd prize?

couldn't see that Betty Grable and June Haver in *The Dolly Sisters* were objects to be worshipped. Perhaps school would iron out the foibles. I went to the local grade school, Principal Sparling, ruled over by a Mr Florence, known as Flossie to the kids.

I did very well; I was very bright and always came first or second in class, alternating with two clever little girls. When I was in the third grade, aged eight, I was taught by a lovely lady called Miss Nina Tessler, a super, warm, inspiring lady who must have spotted something in this weird little boy. She called my mother into school and informed her that this child should have something to do with the arts. 'I don't know what branch of the arts but he must do something!!'

Mother was not at all pleased with this prognosis. She had decided that, with my grades, I was going to become a lawyer and make lots of money and support the family in their old age. She thought she'd better do something, however, so she asked all her friends for suggestions. One of them, who was a fellow curler – (the Scottish sport, very popular in Canada, rather like lawn bowling on ice) – knew Gweneth Lloyd and Betty Farrally who, ten years earlier, had started the Winnipeg Ballet School in the city. 'He seems to have a lot of energy. Why don't you see if he would take to dancing?'

So Mother duly took me along to the ballet school and I watched a men's class. I was struck dumb. These people could leap and turn and jump and not fall over, as I tended to do. This, I decided, at age eight, was what I was going to do for the rest of my life. The decision being firmly made, nothing but *nothing* was ever allowed to stand in the way of its fulfilment. I was jeered, I was teased, I was laughed at and it didn't bother me in the slightest. It must have infuriated potential bullies, including my older brother, that I never rose to the bait. I wasn't made unhappy by this, I just knew that this was my destiny and nothing could deter me. There was certainly nothing in my family's background to prepare for this unusual event...a boy in the 1940s, on the prairies in the mid-west of Canada, embarking on a career in the ballet of all things. In the vernacular of the times, Heavens to Betsy!!

My mother's ancestors were very hardy people who had been in Canada for several generations. In 1800 my great-great-grandfather, Kenneth McBain, was born in Balnigorvan in Rosshire, Scotland. He first emigrated to Nova Scotia, made his way a little west to Ontario and then made the final push to Manitoba in 1861. He and Elizabeth Urquhart had four sons and ten daughters. One of the daughters, Cecilia, grew up to marry William Gair, who became my great-grandparents. It nearly all ended in tragedy, however. The trek west with her family in 1861 when Cecilia was seventeen brushed with disaster. One account has the family travelling in a covered wagon train, another via ox-cart, which doesn't sound quite so romantic. They journeyed west from Ontario through the northern states, got as far as Minnesota and ran smack bang into the last great Sioux rebellion when

Miss Tessler and her brood, 1945. I'm front row fifth from the left.

the Sioux massacred 700 white settlers. In one report, Cecilia's parents missed this by sneaking out with another family in the middle of the night while the whole wagon train was wiped out as they made their way north into Canada. In the other account, they missed it by a day. Whatever, there is no doubt that there were huge numbers killed and I owe my existence to their courage and fortitude. The family settled in Portage la Prairie, a little town in Manitoba.

Cecilia and William, who had also come from Ontario, produced Alexander Gair, who married my grandmother, Eda Alicia Wilson in 1895. They also sired a huge family of twelve children. One son died in infancy, but the surviving family numbered seven girls and four boys. The fifth child was my mother, Elizabeth Mae, born in 1902. Mother and her six sisters were the toast of Portage as young women, ruling the socials and dances of the times. Among the young bucks who came courting was one Patrick Owen McIntyre. Bessie finally succumbed to his charms as they circled arm-in-arm round an ice rink and they were married in 1923.

The McIntyres were not from the same tough pioneering stock as the McBain/Gairs. Indeed, Grandpa McIntyre was a remittance man who was sent over from England in disgrace. He came from a line of very respectable doctors. In 1800, the same year Kenneth McBain was born in Balnigorvan, my paternal great-great-grandfather, Patrick McIntyre, was born in Paisley. He trained as a surgeon at Edinburgh University. On graduating, he came down to Bury St Edmunds in England to work in the new hospital there. He settled, prospered, married Frances Elizabeth Nunn and duly produced the seemingly requisite twelve children. Meanwhile, he found time to serve as Mayor of Bury, edited the *Bury and Suffolk Herald* and became the Governor of the new model gaol, later inspected by the Czar of Russia.

His eldest son, Patrick, was born in 1827. He followed his father into medicine after graduating from King's College, Cambridge. He married a local lady called Rosa Jane Chilton and they had a more modest family, amongst whom was my grandfather, Owen, born in 1864. My great-grandfather had amassed a considerable amount of money by this time, but Grandfather Owen proceeded, as soon as he could lay his hands on any of it, to gamble it away. There were also rumours that he had an affair with a famous actress of the time and was sent to Canada in disgrace, although his daughter, Isobel, always insisted it was because of a government scheme offering financial incentives to open up the Canadian west. He never really got on with Canada and I have memories of him standing on windswept corners, immaculately dressed – a very dapper little man with a cane – but no money. He married Isabella Stewart Pennycook in 1889 and, as well as three girls, had my father, Patrick Owen, in 1900.

Father then grew up with nothing and, when World War 1 broke out, enlisted, lied about his age, and went over as a bugle boy in the Lord Strathcona Horse Regiment when he was fifteen. He went all through the war with barely a scratch, although various friends died horrifically around him, but was finally laid low by the great 'flu epidemic of 1918 and invalided home. Of course he was still only seventeen, so he started with the Canadian Pacific Railways as a messenger boy and stayed with them till he ended up being Controller of Traffic for the western region. After statutory retirement he kept working at various jobs until he was eighty. He was a wonderful man, but the extraordinary thing about him was his attitude towards a war pension. He had, after all, survived those three horrific years. He would never accept one, however. Mother used to roll her eyes at this – she was a more practical person than father, especially when times were hard, but father's view always was 'You don't accept money for doing your duty'.

I suppose one can recognise inherited traits from both sides of the family when they are laid out in black and white. I would like to think I've inherited the Gairs' stubbornness and fortitude possibly mixed with some McIntyre idealism, but the interest in the rather outré aesthetics of the ballet world remains a mystery. However, I started training in 1944, initially with a class once a week on Saturday afternoons. This quickly progressed to private lessons with Miss Lloyd after school. I worked obsessively and drove everyone mad by constantly practising day and night. The training was strict Royal Academy of Dance leavened by lessons in the Greek revival style learned by Gweneth from Ginner Mawer in England. This rather curious combination gave the Winnipeg dancers of my generation a rather exceptional technique. Our RAD placement and technical development was sternly overseen by Betty Farrally, a fierce ballet mistress, but we also had a freedom and joy in movement engendered by the Greek classes. We could run! This supposedly simple feat proved sadly lacking in fellow dancers later on in my career.

For now, it was simply buckling down to two years' hard work to progress in this alien world. Then it was announced that Miss Lloyd was choreographing a new ballet for the 1946 season's performances at the Playhouse Theatre. Formerly on the Pantages circuit and thus visited by everyone from Laurel and Hardy to Pavlova, the Playhouse is a proper old theatre, still standing although now with a modern foyer extension. The ballet was to be called *Pleasure Cruise* about a disparate group of people on a day's river excursion in the 1880s. The family on board was to include three children, one of whom was to be me! The company was just beginning to become semi-professional and I was to receive the grand sum of $5.00.

I was ecstatic. I now added proper rehearsals to my after-school lessons and thus in 1946, aged ten, I started the big adventure.

Chapter Two

I STILL REMEMBER that amazing adrenaline rush as I made my first entrance in *Pleasure Cruise* all those years ago. I never suffered from stage fright – that came much, much later. When you're a child – right up to young adulthood – you're convinced you can do anything and on you go with excitement, but not nerves. A legend grew up many years later when I was dancing in the West End that, because I'd started performing so young, I'd somehow acquired my technique by osmosis, but it wasn't true. The performances in those early days were very few and far between – perhaps once or twice a year we would do a short season at the Playhouse. The months in between were filled with tough struggles with classical technique. I managed to pass my Elementary RAD exam before tours and performances became so invasive that I hadn't enough time for the work involved in preparing for formal examinations.

One of the problems I had in those years was sudden periods of rapid growth. Dame Ninette de Valois, on a visit from England, watched one of our classes. She walked around looking at us all doing our exercises at the barre and remarked, in my hearing, 'That little boy's going to grow too tall – I can tell by the length of his thigh bones.' First of all I was devastated – I thought it was a remarkably cruel thing to say in front of an aspiring dancer. Secondly I thought it was a ridiculous remark when, back home in England, Beryl Grey was towering over all the available male partners of her generation.

There were periods during my teens, however, when it was difficult to maintain the strength needed commensurate with whatever height I was at the time. I would shoot up suddenly and be very skinny for a period. I was practically force fed with bananas and milk shakes to pile on some weight. However, I eventually grew into my strength and never got taller than six feet, which I think is reasonable for a *danseur noble* and certainly became an advantage when I turned to commercial dance later on in my career.

During those early teens there was, of course, one other little problem of a delicate nature. Miss Lloyd had to deputise one of the male members of the company to explain to me that the time had come for me to start wearing a dance belt underneath my tights. The dance belt is a piece of engineering torture designed to smooth out one's nether regions into a non-threatening lump and disguise any unsightly protuberances. It can be agony after wearing one for a long day but it does its job both aesthetically and in providing support while lifting one's partner. I have often wondered why athletes don't adopt the dance belt. The swinging lunch-box effect might have its attractions to some, but I would have thought they could pick up a good second on a 100 metres sprint, say, if they were more streamlined in the genital region!

From my first performance in 1946 through to 1954, when a devastating fire brought a temporary halt to the proceedings, I was growing up both physically and technically, moving from children's roles such as the little black lamb in Miss Lloyd's version of *Façade Suite* – (I'm told I shook my little tail most effectively) – to fully-fledged corps de ballet roles. I played Lust in a ballet called *Visages* before I knew the meaning of the word. At the same time the company itself was growing and becoming more and more professional. From small provincial tours to major forays across the country, its reputation was spreading rapidly. It was further enhanced when it received its Royal Charter in 1952 after performing to the then Princess Elizabeth the year before.

The early pioneering tours of the Winnipeg Ballet were quite remarkable. How some of the towns were persuaded that they needed a ballet company to come and dance for them remains a mystery. The first jaunt I remember was up north to Three Rivers and Churchill. Three Rivers is an army camp, miles up in Northern Manitoba, and Churchill is actually on the fringe of the Arctic Circle. We flew up in sub-zero temperatures and played for these people, who seemed very appreciative, if a trifle bemused. Perhaps they were starved of

Touring at fifteen. I'm on the left of the train steps.

entertainment of any kind. We were treated with extreme courtesy and entertained royally.

The longer tours were by train. The distances, of course, are vast. From Winnipeg to Toronto seems at least equal to the distance between England and Toronto, and it is the same again to get to the West Coast. We would often travel on sleeper Pullman cars as in the movie *Some Like it Hot*. The depiction of the clandestine traffic between upper berths is quite accurate. The difference when we toured in the 1950s, however, was that tiny waists and crinolines were fashionable. Each girl in the company, therefore, had at least seven highly starched unpackable petticoats hung outside her berth. Making one's way down the carriage between the forest of scratchy froth was a nightmare.

One time we were touring in British Columbia. In the early days the company toured with two pianists rather than an unaffordable full orchestra. We were travelling into the interior of British Columbia by bus and going for miles and miles and miles through the mountains and valleys. As we got further and further away from civilisation, the two distinguished American pianists touring with us spent the entire time wondering, audibly, what on earth they were going to have to play on when we finally got to where ever it was we were going. We did eventually arrive and it seemed literally to be a one-horse town as in the Western movies. The only visible sign of life was a Native walking down the middle of the main drag.

The performance venue, however, proved to be a recently built school with a perfectly decent auditorium and a reasonable stage but no sign of pianos. The pianists in some trepidation asked the manager who was there to greet us, 'What are we going to play on?' They were taken behind the stage and there, in an air-conditioned, humidified room, were two Bechstein grands, perfectly tuned and ready to go.

You just never knew what to expect.

I combined the early short tours with my schoolwork. By the time I was fifteen, I was enrolled in St Paul's College, a highly respectable Jesuit high school (Grade Ten – pre-university). My family was not Catholic but mother still had her dreams of me becoming a high-flying lawyer. When the Catholic kids had their devotional period, I went off to study and everything was fine. I would do the tours, come back, catch up and not have any problems. However, when a major trans-Canada tour was announced, I decided I couldn't do both, so I went to the headmaster and said to him, 'Father, I don't think I can combine my career with my school work any more.' All I can remember him saying was, 'Ah, yes, my son – well, travel is educational.' It took me days to break the news to my poor parents, but there it was – I was off on tour and that was that.

As the ballet season ran from September to May, we had the summers to contend with. As a child I had been happily going on summer vacations to my lovely aunts on their farms and up to Delta on the lake but now, after my grand gesture, I felt I had to earn a living. Accordingly, I went west to Vancouver to do summer stock. Theatre under the Stars, which is still going strong, plays in a beautiful, natural amphitheatre in Stanley Park. We would do four major musicals over the summer. Starting in May we would rehearse for a couple of weeks and then run the first two shows for a fortnight each, the third for three weeks and the final one for the four weeks of August. That first year (*New Moon*, *Sweethearts*, *Brigadoon* and *Oklahoma*) was a revelation. The workload was unrelenting. These were full-scale productions and you had to play one at night while rehearsing for two or more of the others all day. Because the season was continuous, the dress rehearsal of the next show took place following the last curtain calls of the previous one.

You would go back to your dressing room while the set was struck and the second act set of the next show erected. You always dress rehearsed the second act first because that was the one that would be seen in darkness and the lighting could be set. You would work all that night and most of the Sunday, come back for a final technical call on the Monday and open that night. Somehow I don't see many of the modern unions buying those working practices.

The performance standards were remarkably high. The producer/choreographer, a lady called Aida Broadbent, (who incidentally had a photographic memory; she would come back from Broadway with an entire production imprinted on her mind – very useful, if a trifle unethical) had various friends and connections in Hollywood. This resulted in people from the film world coming up the coast to try something different. For instance, we had Terry Saunders come to play the title role in *Annie Get Your Gun*. She had just filmed *The King and I* with Yul Brynner and Deborah Kerr, playing the first wife where she sang 'Something Wonderful' charmingly. She wanted a contrast to such a dutiful, submissive role and so came up to us to let off steam playing Annie Oakley. Those were happy summers, particularly in August when there were no daytime rehearsals. There was an arcane insurance rule cancelling the evening performance if a specified amount of rain fell between five and six in the evening, but despite our vigorous rain dances at 4.59 p.m. we seldom had a night off!

It was during my second summer season that the ghastly fire of 1954 wiped out a good deal of downtown Winnipeg, taking with it the company's studio along with all its artefacts. I therefore stayed in Vancouver and started in the new medium that had just arrived, television. I danced in a variety programme called *Parade* and spent the winter appearing in flickering black and white. Those very early live television appearances were fairly hit and miss. Later, in Winnipeg, I had a series called *Steps in Time* that involved a partner and me giving a lecture demonstration followed by a pas de deux in every style from classical ballet to French Apache dance. The latter became one of the

With Kay Bird as Vernon and Irene Castle on early Canadian television.

misses when my partner's skirt was torn off during one of our more passionate encounters. There's very little that can be done to rectify such a situation when the programme is live, except grin and bare it.

In the autumn of 1955 the Royal Winnipeg Ballet was reformed and I was asked to rejoin the company. This time, however, I was to be a principal dancer. All those years of effort were paying off. I couldn't have been more delighted. I was nineteen. The new company was to be re-shaped by the American dancer Ruthanna Boris, assisted by her husband, Frank Hobi. Miss Boris was Balanchine trained and started out by taking our techniques to a new degree of polish and profes-sionalism. She was a very fine teacher and an interesting choreographer. She did several ballets for the new company and I danced the lead in

A principal at last!

her first major work, *Pasticcio*. That was great fun. Also with the company was a ballet master, Nenad Lhotka, who was a refugee from Yugoslavia. He staged a version of a Yugoslav folk-ballet called *Devil in the Village*. His father, Franz, had written the music for it twenty years before. I was to play the title role.

The ballet, particularly in those days, was a very hierarchical world and one worked one's way painstakingly up through the ranks. I had, of course, started as a child and then worked up through the corps de ballet. The rite of passage involved in becoming a principal, however, was immensely satisfying. When I arrived for my first rehearsal of *Devil in the Village*, Mr Lhotka – who was also very much of the old school – said to one of the corps de ballet members, 'Would you get Mr

McIntyre a chair, please.' I was thrilled. Even I can see how ludicrous that seems at this distance, but at the time it felt like receiving an Oscar.

The new company worked very well and after a successful season in Winnipeg we embarked on much more elaborate and longer tours, including going down to the States. The following season we had Alicia Markova over as guest artiste. She appeared in Winnipeg and toured down to Washington as well. The first time we saw her she arrived in a black Dior form-fitting suit with a hat and gloves and extremely high heels. She looked the epitome of glamour to us provincial types. She did *Les Sylphides* with us as well as two solos – her 'Dying Swan' and a very popular little Spanish solo.

She brought her sister, Doris Barry, who was a very successful production manager for Hughie Greene on television for many years, to help with lighting cues etc. When Madame Markova did the 'Dying Swan', she would arrive in the theatre several hours before the performance and sit facing the mirror in her dressing room to allow the mantle of Pavlova to fall. One night the mantle had fallen as per schedule and all went well until the climax of the piece. At the very end the poor swan sinks to the floor with her right leg extended in front of her, arches back, has one last long fluttering of the arms and then folds them forward over the extended leg. There is a final little flutter and the upper hand drops to the stage with a gentle thud, which is the cue for the blackout. Miss Barry was in the lighting box to give the cue and, unfortunately, gave the blackout cue a beat too soon, before the poor dead hand had fallen to the stage. Apparently, she went as white as a sheet, ran backstage and locked herself in the loo under the stage. The next thing we observed was the swan flying down the stairs in full rage, screaming, 'Where is she? Where is she?' On discovering her sister's whereabouts, she proceeded to try to kick the door down with her pointe shoes, which, stiffened with shellac, made a horrendous din. She pounded and pounded and used language that I don't think I've ever heard from a swan before. Wise Miss Barry stayed there long enough for the fury to subside and all was more or less well again. Professionally, Dame Alicia might have been a perfectionist (she had been known to hiss to the stage crew while performing that the wrong gelatine was in the fourth light on the third bar from the right) and not miss a beat, but she had a wonderfully generous spirit.

With Marina Katronis in the Don Quixote *pas de deux.*

It was the year, in the fifties, when nylon net became available. The tutus in the romantic ballets like *Les Sylphides* are knee to ankle length and, before nylon net was invented, were layers of tarlatan. Dame Alicia arrived with her own costume and of course it was made with the new net that looked brighter – it was a different shade of white compared to the tarlatan of everyone else's. To her enormous credit, Dame Alicia contacted England and had sent over enough nylon net to make a top layer for all the other girls in the ballet, which I thought was charming of her. She is a lovely lady, Dame Alicia, still alive and as elegant as ever.

I now took on the great classic pas de deux. These would be done as excerpts in a mixed evening of ballets. The company still lacked the resources to stage the full length classics, but I danced the *Nutcracker*

With the corps de ballet in Pasticcio.

and the *Sleeping Beauty* grand pas de deux with the lovely Marilyn Young, who like me had grown up in the company, the 'Pas de Trois' from *Swan Lake* and the *Don Quixote* pas de deux with Marina Katronis. Both Marina and I were 'turners' which meant we could pirouette endlessly. Accordingly, David Adams, originally with the company, came back from abroad and choreographed *Masquerade* for us to the Khachaturyan waltz, which was insanely difficult technically, perhaps a bit circus horsy, but undoubtedly effective. Paddy Stone, who had left for England the year I began training, also returned to do *Classico*, a ballet for four couples to South American rhythms.

I no longer had to go to Vancouver for the summers, as Winnipeg had its own version called Rainbow Stage, and I plunged into leading

Solo from Aurora's Wedding.

musical comedy roles, notably Scarecrow in the *Wizard of Oz*. Everything was fine and I was busy and successful, although I did have a sneaking feeling that I was in danger of becoming a large fish in a small pond. There was also some internal politics in the company that forced out Miss Boris. The proposal was to make Mrs Farrally Artistic Director. I wrote a confidential resignation letter to the Board giving my reasons for not agreeing with the new order. I felt she had been a marvellous Ballet Mistress and I owed her a great deal, but didn't feel her qualities were suitable for an Artistic Director. A few months later this letter was to have surprising repercussions. For now, though, I had no regrets and set out to try the wide world.

Accordingly, I flew to New York, auditioned for American Ballet

Theatre, was accepted immediately and arranged to meet them on tour in Hollywood in a month's time after arranging my visa. Lucia Chase, the legendary founder of ABT was very flattering after watching me take company class, insinuating that various roles were just around the corner and that I was the 'classical hope for the company'. Burying thoughts that I should have waited for Balanchine to get back to town to audition for the rival New York City Centre Company, which would have suited my style more accurately, I flew home to arrange things. The chap at the visa office, however, warned me that I would be swept up into the Korean draft with an ordinary working visa. Luckily he was a fan, recognised me and dug in his desk for an H1 Petition, which is for a Worker of Outstanding Merit and Ability (I've always thought it sounded like a Soviet Peace Prize) that gave me immunity.

Armed with my protective visa I therefore flew on the Champagne Flight from Minneapolis to Hollywood to start on the next stage of my career. I had just turned twenty-one.

By the way, have I mentioned that by this time I'd also acquired a wife and two children?

Chapter 3

EARLY ON IN MY first season as a soloist in 1955, I arrived at the studio to find a blonde woman crawling about the floor on her hands and knees.

She was wearing jeans and a man's denim shirt tied at the waist and was marking out the floor plan for the ballet to be rehearsed. This was Peggy Green, well known in the city for her acting and directing, who had been persuaded by her old friends, Gweneth and Betty, to stage-manage the forthcoming tour. Peg at this point was thirty-four years old with two children of ten and eight. I was a callow youth of nineteen. At first sight, it seemed highly unlikely that we were destined to spend the next thirty-five years together.

Born Margaret Inger Jarman in 1921, Peg was an astonishing woman. Her parents, Robert Jarman and Bertha Knowles, had met at the turn of the century when they were in Denmark studying the new callisthenics which were fashionable at that time. Peg's middle name, Inger, reflects the Scandinavian influence. Bertha came from a rather wealthy cotton family and there was some suggestion that she was marrying beneath her. Robert, however, was an energetic and a very talented man. In the late 1920s, he was asked over to Canada to organise physical education in the Canadian schools. He stationed himself in Winnipeg, it being right in the centre of the country, and was very successful. He was also a remarkably good amateur actor and director and did a great deal to start the fledgling dramatic societies in the town, which grew to export some very talented people both across Canada and down to the States.

Peg and her parents had been living outside Liverpool – in a house called West Hall, a beautiful place that Peg and I found again very late in her life (we managed to track it down and spent a lovely day in her old

Dear Peg.

environs) – when she was taken to Canada aged six. To her, it was always the great tragedy of her life. She never got over being torn away, as she saw it, from England. Her brother Robert, known as Trant, adapted very successfully to the North American continent. When he grew up he went south to the States, became an American citizen and raced cars, wrote on the subject for glossy magazines and participated in the Monte Carlo rally.

Peg, with her mother, spent her early years trailing back and forth across the Atlantic by boat, to prep school down in Devon for a while and then back again when she was sixteen, when she won a place at the Old Vic School in London – she had found her niche. Tyrone Guthrie had just taken over the company after Lilian Baylis's death and Peg found herself playing a fairy in his famous production of *A Midsummer Night's Dream* starring Vivien Leigh and Robert Helpmann. The following summer, 1939, when she was seventeen, the Vic played a season up at the Buxton Opera House. Peg was taken along as one of two assistant stage managers.

They were playing two productions, *Romeo and Juliet* and *The Devil's Disciple*, starring Robert Donat and Constance Cummings in a company that included, amongst other distinguished players, Max Adrian and Stewart Grainger (with his original name of Jimmy Stewart, which he obviously had to change when he got to Hollywood). Everything was going fine until, of course, in September, war was declared. All the theatres in London were immediately closed so the question was what to do with the Old Vic Company. Finally it was decided to send it on the road.

These two productions had very heavy sets, made for the London theatre, not for touring, but they managed to lumber around the country. However, as they progressed, all the men backstage, one by one, went away to enlist until finally Peg, at seventeen, found herself the Stage Manager of this unlikely tour. She took a deep breath, plunged in and found herself liking the responsibility, and had a splendid time. When the tour finished, she was asked by Esme Church to go to Edinburgh, where a joint repertory was being set up between Glasgow and Edinburgh, to play one week alternately in each town. She was getting on very well – this was a very good career move for someone of that age.

However, by that time, as the war was getting more and more serious, her parents panicked and ordered her back yet again to Winnipeg. Once home, she took on another man's job, as it were, and became Night Editor of the *Winnipeg Free Press*, getting the news of the battles and casualties over the wires, surrounded by boys and by men who were too old to go to war. She also took over some of her father's directing duties and ran her own theatre for a time. She played in some highly successful performances of her own; a remarkable *Medea* in particular drew high praise. She played everything from classical Greek tragedy to Bloody Mary in *South Pacific*.

She had married a chap called Aubrey Green and they collaborated in writing radio scripts, serials, soaps and plays. She also sold to the American *Ellery Queen Mystery Magazine*. More importantly, of course, they produced what were to become my wonderful stepchildren. By the time I came along, however, Aubrey had rather succumbed to the drink and was living in Toronto. The reason she was asked to stage-manage the ballet company stemmed from the fact that the Jarmans were old friends of Gweneth Lloyd and her partner, Betty Farally. They had run a dancing school in Leeds (even attempting to teach a rebellious Peg at one point). Dear Peg could never quite see the point of the dance, or musicals, for that matter, which makes our liaison all the more surprising. When Betty and Gweneth decided to come to Canada to seek new opportunities, they travelled across the country and got as far as Winnipeg and stopped, simply because the Jarmans were there. They had somewhere where they knew somebody and that's where they set up the ballet school, which eventually became the Royal Winnipeg Ballet. So, there were wheels within wheels within wheels…

Peg and I and the company started out on that major tour in 1955 and somehow she and I found ourselves in corners laughing at the world, the company, ourselves, whatever. Perhaps it was hysteria brought on by overtiredness. The tour was tough, particularly for her. We played an old theatre in Vancouver, for instance, that had been a cinema for thirty years. Her first job was to clear the flies. The first thing to come down along with clouds of choking dust was the set for *Uncle Tom's Cabin*!

As Peg and I became inseparable, Betty found herself involved in various schemes she couldn't quite approve of. As part of management Peg was entitled to a Stateroom on the train while I, a mere principal, was due a lower berth. As the Stateroom slept two, Betty simply left me off the train roster hoping no one would notice. Naturally, all the members of the corps de ballet came to her one by one and, wide-eyed, asked her, 'Where is Paddy going to sleep? Ooh, Mrs Farrally, you've forgotten Paddy!' She was not amused.

The last night of the tour stretched my capacity to laugh to the limit. We were playing *Devil in the Village* in Regina, Saskatchewan. The climax of the ballet has the hero trick me, as the Devil, into touching a cross in the graveyard. As I did, an electric charge passed through a tin of gunpowder concealed at the base of the cross. There was a loud explosion and a cloud of smoke. When it cleared both the cross and the wicked devil had disappeared into the wings. There were two problems that night in Regina, however. One, the wings in Darke Hall are tiny. Two, the props department decided it would be easier to use up all the remaining gunpowder rather than having to account for the leftovers to the Royal Canadian Mounted Police.

It had been going very well and I was emoting my little heart out. I whirled around, touched the cross and suddenly World War III broke out. There was an enormous bang and clouds of billowing smoke. I leapt into the wing, the cross followed but the bloody thing kept exploding. I couldn't get away from it. I was trapped in a tiny space, dancing about like a cowboy being shot at in a Western movie. It didn't help that, peering through the clearing smoke, I spotted my beloved in the opposite wing doubled over in helpless laughter.

Back home we decided to try living together. Our main concern was how the children would react. Hilary was then ten and David eight. To our astonishment they both appeared to take it in their stride. From the beginning I've had a close and loving relationship with both my step-children. When our son, Patrick, was born later in England, we cohered into an extremely tight-knit family united against the world, with Peg as a benevolent matriarch. Before Peg and I could marry there had, of course, to be a divorce (also I had to have reached the currently legal age of twenty-one). Peg and Aubrey had agreed a very civilised arrangement whereby he would provide the physical evidence and Peg would divorce him. In those days, of course, you had to have actual physical evidence of adultery; there was no other way to obtain a decree.

After we had been living together in Winnipeg for, I suppose, about six or eight months, Aubrey came to town and went out with a bunch of the press boys. He got roaring drunk and persuaded them to come round to Peg's. They burst in, came upstairs, our bedroom door flew open and there was Aubrey and various pressmen with those large, old-fashioned flash press cameras, taking pictures of the two of us in bed. Peg was totally outraged and jumped out of bed, stark naked, and chased them all down the stairs and out the door while I sat up in bed, ate a banana and contemplated life. Peg expected me to be totally traumatised but I thought it was rather fun; it was like a scene from *The Front Page*. Anyway, that led to my other claim to fame, I suppose. I became named as the youngest divorce co-respondent in the history of the Manitoba Law Courts! Everything went through very easily, except that of course the shoe was on the other foot. It was Aubrey who divorced Peg rather than the other way round.

In the summer of 1957, a week after my twenty-first birthday, we were doing Summer Stock at Rainbow Stage. This was its second

The unlikely couple.

season. The opening production was *Can Can*. I was playing the Snake in the Garden of Eden ballet and Peg was directing. On the day of the opening night, we finished the technical rehearsal at about four in the afternoon and having managed to make an appointment (the only time we could get) with the Register Office in town, called a halt to rehearsals, got into some nice clothes, grabbed a couple of witnesses, got married and rushed back for the opening. Both witnesses were later to have highly distinguished careers in their respective fields – Arnold Spohr, who was to take over the Artistic Direction of the Royal Winnipeg and Bill McPherson, who rose to the editorship of a national newspaper. It wasn't a very romantic occasion but it served its purpose and we were blissfully happy.

It was at the end of this summer season in 1957 that I bid the family a temporary farewell and flew down to Hollywood. By an extraordinary coincidence the American Ballet Theatre tour was coming up the West Coast from Hollywood to Vancouver and then crossing Canada to Winnipeg. I would therefore be back playing my hometown, albeit with a new company, and able to pick up my loved ones all within the space of a month.

Chapter 4

*Sunshine, palm trees and Giselle…the extraordinary Nora Kaye…
the sublime Eric Bruhn…Nora, Lucia and the Winnipeg reporter
…one night stands…apartheid in the Deep South…chicken pox!…
State Department tour of Europe*

LANDING AMONGST the sunshine and palm trees was quite a thrill for someone from the 'frozen north', but I didn't have much time to admire the scenery. One of the boys had sprained an ankle and I was thrown on in *Giselle* that same night. Luckily, the men only appear in the first act and the corps de ballet choreography is relatively straight-forward, so learning an entire ballet in an afternoon is not quite as onerous as might be expected. What was astonishing, however, was witnessing Nora Kaye's mad scene at close quarters. I had never seen an artist with such single-minded concentration and conviction, coupled with the ability to convey emotion with such raw honesty. The audience was gripped, as was I on stage. It was almost too painful to watch.

Although American Ballet Theatre turned out not to be a happy experience for me professionally, (I should have listened to that inner voice saying 'Wait for Balanchine!') I shall always be grateful for the chance to witness and learn from many remarkable dancers at the peak of their form. This was the last great flowering of Ballet Theatre when many of their groundbreaking works were still being performed by the original artists. Nora was a prime example. Giselle was not in fact one of her best roles; she lacked the ethereal quality needed for the second act, but to see her in Agnes de Mille's *Fall River Legend*, for instance, was a revelation. Most roles, whether in ballet or the theatre in general, are capable of a myriad of interpretations and subsequent revivals can be extremely successful, but occasionally a role created for a particular performer remains definitive.

This was certainly one of them, and jumping forward in time for a moment, so was Chita Rivera's Anita in *West Side Story*. Watching Miss Moreno's performance in the film version was like watching Chita's through the wrong end of a telescope, despite her Oscar. Back to Ballet Theatre. There was John Kriza, for whom Jerome Robbins had created *Fancy Free*, which subsequently became the basis for the musical *On the Town*. There were the classic technicians such as Lupe Serrano and Scott Douglas, the charming French ballerina Violette Verdy, and above all there was Eric Bruhn. Eric was probably as near as perfect a classical dancer as is possible to produce. His line was elegant and perfectly placed, his jump was effortless and landings deep and soft.

[NON – DANCERS CAN SKIP THIS NEXT BIT!]

I watched from the wings while he did the male solo from the Black Swan pas de deux one night. He did three slow *en dedan* pirouettes in *a la seconde* at hip height, stopped facing front on a high demi-pointe and slowly turned into an *arabesque fondu* with the leg rotating perfectly in the hip socket, staying at exactly hip height.

Sorry, non-dancers, but this is the hole-in-one, the ninety-yard touchdown pass, the perfect ten, and I felt obliged to record it.

Back to me. It turned out that the extravagant promises of future parts made to me at my audition had been leaked to the company. Moreover, all the roles in question had been expected to go to a very popular senior member of the corps de ballet and this made me an extremely unpopular upstart from the north. I was definitely not flavour of the month. However, I kept my head down, learned the corps roles and looked forward to getting back to Winnipeg. The buzz in town regarding our wedding had pretty well died down by now. Ours was the only marriage of the year to make the front page rather than the society column. The predictions as to how long we'd last ranged from ten minutes to a few months. Nevertheless, the family were all packed and ready to move on to New York after we finished our performances in Winnipeg.

On the opening night, however, I had a most curious conversation with Nora Kaye. She and Lucia Chase had given an interview to the local newspaper arts correspondent. It was a splendid opportunity for him to ask questions of a prima ballerina and the founder of one of the great ballet companies, or so you'd think. According to Nora, however, he spent the entire time instead telling them to be careful of me, that they mustn't trust me, as I would undoubtedly betray them in the end. Miss Kaye was totally bemused but the explanation was simple. That confidential resignation letter I'd sent to the Board had been shown to Mrs Farrally who had shown it in turn to her dear friend, the reporter. Whether it actually did me harm is debatable. The explanation finally given to me for my lack of progress was that the European tour was being arranged and that the theatres overseas had insisted on all the modern American works like *Rodeo*, *Billy the Kid*, *Fall River Legend*, *Fancy Free*, etc. at the expense of the classics. I ended up playing the Postman in *Billy the Kid*. Any dancer of my generation knows that once cast in that part, you're dead.

After a big delayed wedding party, we all headed for New York for a rehearsal period, before hitting the road again. Most of the company not based in the city stayed at the Dauphin Hotel on Broadway, later torn down to make way for Lincoln Centre. It was a theatrical 'apartment hotel' which meant it had a cupboard with a hot plate allowing some rudimentary cooking. It was cheap at $35 per week. We, of course, needed two rooms and that came to $50 per week. There was one slight problem, however; the rehearsal salary at that time was precisely $50 per week. The idea was that you made extra money on tour to subsidize yourself during rehearsals. The profligate starved. Not for the last time did Peg's talent for whipping up nourishing meals from virtually nothing come to the fore. Somehow we survived, I was off on tour, and the family moved back to a single room and arranged to visit me at strategic points on the road.

Touring with American Ballet Theatre, however, was a much more serious affair than with the Canadian company, harder work and much less fun. It was also a much bigger operation. We would tour with two alternating sets of performances so that the crew would be sent ahead to set up one lot of four ballets in one town while we danced the alternate programme in another. The towns were anything up to 400 miles apart.

We would get down to the bus, if we were lucky, at nine in the morning, but for really long distances, it was 6 a.m. We'd travel all day, arrive at the next hotel at, say, five in the evening, dump our bags, try to get something quick to eat, dash to the theatre, warm-up, do the performance, try to remember the way back to the hotel and get up at

6 a.m. the next day to do the same things all over again. We would do these one-nighters for stretches of three months at a time. Occasionally, we would have nice dates of two weeks in Chicago, three weeks in Hollywood (we played the open-air Greek Theatre there) or a week in Boston and that was splendid, but these one-night stand gigs went on for three solid, unforgiving months. We did one lot all over the mid-west of the States and another in the Deep South.

It seems extraordinary to remember that such a very short time ago, the Deep South was totally apartheid. For someone who had never had any dealings with black people, the way they were treated down South, with separate washrooms, separate drinking fountains, that sort of thing, was simply astonishing. A couple of us took a bus one afternoon – a perfectly ordinary one-decker bus – that had a red line painted across the floor, about two-thirds of the way back. When we got on, there were plenty of seats in the front section with only a few occupied by white people, but behind the red line was jammed with blacks. There was nothing physically preventing them from occupying the rest of the bus, it was just that red line. Everybody was obeying that arbitrary rule and it just seemed so extraordinary to us.

The other incident I remember very clearly was walking back to the hotel with two of the other boys from the company after a performance. We had lost our way – this was always happening because every town looked exactly the same and you could never remember whether to turn left or right outside the theatre. We were walking down the deserted street, empty except for a young, black boy – maybe seventeen – who was coming towards us and we said, 'Oh good, we'll ask him the way.'

Now remember, these were three male ballet dancers. We were hardly the most threatening types in the world and we were perfectly well-disposed towards this chap but, as one of us said 'Excuse me' and started to speak to him, he jumped off the pavement into the gutter, whipped off his cap, held it close to his chest and said 'Yessa, boss, yessa, boss' and appeared terrified. We all three felt totally devastated by this. It was appalling, absolutely appalling, and I will never forget it. To this day, I find America's high moral posturing a bit unconvincing, given what is to me its very recent history.

Two other occasions stand out in one's memory from travelling round America. One was a lovely week in Boston. The family joined me and we wandered around the city, fed the squirrels on the Common and soaked up its unique atmosphere. I haven't been back to Boston since that spring forty-five years ago, but I do hope it has retained some of that measured calm that set it apart from other more frenetic US towns.

The other memory is not so pleasant. I managed to catch chicken pox in Milwaukee. For some reason I had missed all the normal childhood diseases. No measles, no mumps, no nothing! Maybe I'd been saving up for an almighty infection. If so, this was definitely it. I was covered from head to toe in spots. It was ghastly. Naturally the company panicked, as it couldn't afford to be quarantined, and so came up with a cunning plan. Dump me! Well, not quite. They flew off to the next date while I had strict instructions to stay in my hotel room for a week, order from room service but always be in the shower when the food arrived. When I could be seen in public again, I was to fly on to the next town but one with a hat pulled down over my face and rejoin them. The terrible thing about this heartless, if practical, plan was, it worked!

The State Department had decided to send the company on a goodwill tour of Europe taking in the Brussels World Fair and to act as Ambassadors as the first American company to venture behind the Iron Curtain since the height of the Cold War. Great excitement. I sent Peg and the kids over on a slow boat and we later piled into a turbo-prop aircraft (it took seventeen hours if I remember rightly) to begin this great tour of Europe. What was to be our first date in Europe? Casablanca! Don't ask.

Chapter 5

Off to Casablanca…the family settle in Spain…behind the Iron Curtain…pleas for help in Warsaw…the Bolshoi in Paris…a Canuck in Germany…another disastrous fire…decide to turn commercial

WHOEVER BOOKED the 1958 European tour of the American Ballet Theatre had either never looked at a map or had an extremely quirky sense of humour. We criss-crossed the continent in a totally haphazard manner jumping from places like Dublin to Dubrovnik or Warsaw to the South of France. We somehow managed to play the Brussels World Fair on two separate occasions in the same summer. In a sense it didn't matter in the slightest, for we were young, agog with excitement and took everything in our stride.

The family was waiting to greet the plane in Casablanca and once the company had established that we were in Africa instead of Europe, the mystery tour began. We started on a mini-Moroccan tour playing the aforesaid Casablanca followed by Tangier and Rabat. This was before mass tourism, so the country still retained its essential flavours and essences with no overly Western influence. Tangier particularly was still a Free Port and, although seemingly lawless and amoral on the surface, there was no hassling in the streets and the Moroccans were courteous and welcoming. The Kasbah, despite its lurid reputation, had a curiously homely feel once one was used to the culture shock.

It was decided that the family would spend the summer across the Straits of Gibraltar in Southern Spain while I trailed around Europe. Torremolinos was a tiny, quiet, fishing village in those days with no visitor accommodation, but one of the local grandees had a little villa in the orange grove of his mansion on the mountainside, so Peg and the kids settled in while I set out to bring culture to the natives. All went well for them while I danced in places like France, Belgium, Scandinavia or Germany and the money I sent arrived every week.

Unfortunately, no one had foreseen that when I disappeared behind the Iron Curtain, I'd be unable to get money out. Those oranges (and the British Consul in Gibraltar) were to prove very handy.

At this distance, many of the places and incidents have become decidedly hazy, but some were so bizarre they feel like last week. That Dublin – Dubrovnik hop was very dramatic. This was to be our first Iron Curtain visit, although Tito was perceived as a much gentler proposition than Stalin, for instance. Even so, there was considerable tension evident among members of the company who had been brought up on the evils of communism through years of Cold War rhetoric. The Yugoslavs insisted on using their planes to fly us over and came to Dublin to pick us up. They didn't have one big enough for the whole company, so we divided into two and took off. I was on the first plane, which wasn't very strong on luxuries and none of the crew spoke a word of English, but all seemed fine until we started our descent. Looking out the windows, it became quickly apparent that there was no airport.

We were coming down in mountainous terrain with the sea glinting far below, not onto a runway beside terminus buildings, but rather into a cow pasture with a tin shed at the corner of the field. The corps de ballet naturally leapt to the logical conclusion that we were about to be lined up to be shot, when the rather sullen non-English speaking crew gestured that we were to climb down. As we made our way over to the tin hut, the second plane was seen getting ready to come in and some of the braver souls tried to gesture to it to fly on. 'Go, go, save yourselves.' Nothing worked, however, and soon the entire company was assembled in the tin hut waiting nervously for something to happen. Finally a fleet of buses was seen winding its way up the mountain to take us down to the hotel. It was all a bit of an anti-climax in the end, but everything was forgotten in the astonishment of one's first sight of Dubrovnik. The ancient honey-coloured walled city is truly glorious. More recently when the country was tearing itself apart, the sight of shells destroying centuries of beauty was heartbreaking. It has been rebuilt since, but I don't think I can bring myself to go back in case the patina of age has been lost.

Warsaw was a much more serious proposition. Coming from a land of overflowing bounty, too young to remember the depression, too featherbrained to realize that a whole world existed outside of pirouettes and arabesques, seeing the devastated city centre was a shattering experience. The entire area had been pulverised by persistent bombing and amongst the acres of rubble were long lines of grandmothers patiently picking over the bricks and passing the reusable ones back along the line to be stacked. We were there for three weeks and the lines never seemed to shorten or the stacks of bricks to grow perceptibly.

Right in the centre, however, Stalin had built the People's Palace, which was a gleaming white smaller copy of the Empire State building but with Russian curlicues at the corners. This obscenity was naturally the only postcard vista to be seen in the West. What the people had managed to build themselves was the Warszawa Hotel where we stayed and, amazingly, the Opera House where we danced. The people were wonderful; friendly, outgoing and tremendously enthusiastic about the company and its works. The local ballet company had suffered dreadfully along with everyone else and we could help a little with tights and shoes and the like, but felt increasingly helpless in the face of such overwhelming poverty.

The hotel did its best, but food remained a problem. We were told that the farmers couldn't afford to feed their cows to maturity so we had veal every night. There were simply no fresh vegetables and the only fruits available were tiny wizened apples sold on the street corners by the grandmothers not on brick duty. Some of the visit was pure farce. We were followed every time we ventured out by identikit KGB men in tightly belted black trench coats and fedoras. They walked a regulation twenty paces behind us, stopped when we did and continued on cue. We tried a couple of *grand jetés* to see if they would copy but they remained impassive. No fun at all!

Our waiter at the hotel took to sending us notes concealed under the plates. He had, allegedly, managed to get abroad, settled down, married an English girl and joined the British Merchant Navy. Years later he stepped ashore in a neutral country where he was snatched by Communist agents and whisked back to Poland. He was desperate to get out and pleaded for us to help. Apart from offering sympathy, there was nothing we could possibly do. He was one of many who poured out their desperation to us. Unfortunately, we were more Prince Siegfrieds than James Bonds. Now, if they had been swans…

Arriving back into what we considered civilization, suitably chastened, we played Paris. This could have been disastrous artistically, because the Bolshoi Company was playing there simultaneously. They were at the Opera House while we were at the much smaller Sarah Bernhardt. Some of the critical comparisons were invidious, but due deference was paid to the modern American works, as predicted. Luckily, I got to see the Bolshoi dancing on a night when I wasn't performing. Some other members of the company gave me the evening as a birthday treat. I had a seat in a box at the Paris Opera and Galina Ulanova danced Giselle! This was the Bolshoi while it still had all the opulence and magnitude of sets and costumes that the west hadn't seen for many years. They were wonderfully old-fashioned in the best sense of the word. Madame Ulanova, who must have been in her mid-forties, had a figure like a box of Kleenex, but it didn't matter. She was just enchanting, the most wonderful, powerful actress. It was thrilling.

In the second act of *Giselle*, after her death, Giselle joins the Wilis, who are the ghosts of young women who have died through unrequited love, but it's probably not too wise to concentrate on details of the plot. Suffice it to say, the act opens in a misty glade in the woods with wonderful great trees and ghostly figures flying (literally) across the back. The two-timing hero appears to pray by Giselle's grave, wearing a long cloak and carrying a large bunch of lilies. (Anton Dolin, Markova's partner, wore a cloak so long that the trailing end only appeared on one side of the stage when he had reached the far side, but that's by the by.) While he, Albrecht, kneels by the tomb, the ghost of Giselle appears several times, touches him and disappears before the doomed lovers finally get together to dance, and dance, and dance…

In one appearance, she was perched on a high, high branch of a tree on stage right that, at the appropriate time, bent gracefully down over the stage. It was a perfectly smooth and astonishing mechanical effect. The branch, with her on it, came down, she touched him and then it gracefully went back up again. You had a terrible momentary thought that, as in a slingshot, she might be catapulted off, but she wasn't. It was all very splendid.

We continued rattling around Europe apace, one day marvelling at being able to take walks in the Norwegian mountains at night in the unearthly glow of the midnight sun, another being poured onto the plane after a farewell champagne breakfast in Copenhagen, or to gingerly drink the spa waters in Baden Baden. Most of the varying populations we encountered were incredibly friendly and enthusiastic, but we quickly learned that travelling in Germany at that time presented unique difficulties. We'd had several instances of appallingly rude treatment in German restaurants until one night by chance I happened to wear a Maple Leaf pin on my lapel. On discovering that I was indeed Canadian, everything changed. We were treated like royalty. I never really discovered why Americans were so fiercely resented compared to us saintly Canucks, but the difference was startling. From then on, I prominently wore my pin; the rest of the table kept their mouths shut while I did the ordering and all was well.

Suddenly we were in Paradise. We found ourselves in Cannes on the Riviera. It was late summer, the weather was heavenly, the sea was impossibly blue and we had a week of daytime bliss while performing in a charming little theatre in the evenings. Reluctantly, we gathered for the train call on Sunday morning only to be met by an ashen-faced company manager. He told us that the huge pantechnicon that had been loaded up after our last performance the previous night had caught fire and that everything was gone. Apparently, the driver had made his way over the mountains in dead of night in his separated cab, totally unaware of the fire reducing the enormous trailer behind him to a skeletal framework. All the sets, costumes, props, scores, as well as all our personal trunks were gone.

'I'm afraid,' he said with a distinctly trembling lower lip, 'that you're all going to have to stay here in Cannes for at least three weeks while we try to borrow sets and costumes from the European ballet companies.'

'Aaaaaah! How dreadful! What a shame! Isn't it shocking?…Last one in the water's a sissy'! If the gesture had been invented, we'd have high-fived. Paradise regained.

It couldn't last, of course, and having begged and borrowed costumes and sets to make-do, we set off again to finish the tour. Now that the end was in sight decisions had to be made. The company plan was to have a six-week lay off before a three-week rehearsal period followed by a short season at the old Metropolitan Opera House. This was decidedly unappealing. Rehearsals living on short shrift were one thing but a complete lay off with nothing coming in was ridiculous. Peg had always wanted to get back to England. I felt I'd been touring forever and longed to stay in one place for a while. Something needed to happen.

In another weird coincidence, the tour ended full circle in Santander in Spain. The family came up country to meet us and, after a very brief discussion, the big decision seemed to make itself. I would retire from my career in the ballet world and TURN COMMERCIAL! Gathering my brood and all my Grandma Gair fortitude about me, I waved good-bye to American Ballet Theatre and by bus, train, ferry and train we made our way to the one place in the Western world where you can make films, television and work in top class live theatre all from the same base. London. I was twenty-two.

Chapter 6

Arrival in England…straight into the West End…the kindness of strangers…from stage turkey to risky television…West Side Story on the horizon

WE ARRIVED AT Euston Station on a Friday afternoon in September 1958. I had a wife, two children and £2.10s. in my pocket. The first sight of the English en masse was not very promising. Having spent three weeks frolicking in the South of France amongst the glitterati, the contrast was startling. The English seemed grey, careworn and depressed by comparison. Not surprising after all those years of war and rationing, but I very quickly fell in love with these generous-hearted people and their stunning country.

I had one telephone number to try, the Winnipeg choreographer Paddy Stone, who had preceded me over the water and was having a successful time over here. I deposited my tuppence, pressed Button A and told Paddy I had arrived. 'Oh good, I'm starting a new West End musical on Monday, come in and start rehearsing.' So that was all right.

There was a flat-finding agency called Centicom in Euston. Peg picked Kew Green as a nice place to live and they sent us down there (by double decker bus with the conductor calling me Guv). I was enchanted. I dropped off the family and went to see the bank manager on the High Street who gave me £50 on the 'pay us back when you can' principle. Is it any wonder I adore this extraordinary country? Mind you, although I only had the famous £2.10s., I did have some expectations. I was promised $900 insurance money for our personal effects from the ABT fire, and I was to start work on Monday. However, I had no tangible proof of any of this. All those wonderful people accepted one on trust. No sureties, no deposits, no collateral.

I reported for duty on Monday to find Paddy was co-choreographing the show with his partner, Irving Davies. This was to prove very useful once the show had closed, which wasn't very long in coming. The turkey was called *Mr Venus* written by Norman Newell, the record producer, and Trevor Stanford, before he became famous as Russ Conway, the pianist. It was supposed to be a vehicle for Norman Wisdom who had dropped out and had been replaced by Frankie Howerd. This was just before Frankie's slide into oblivion before being resurrected, a few years later, at the Establishment Club. We rehearsed for five weeks, went out on the road for five weeks, came into the West End to the Prince of Wales Theatre and ran for ten days. Anton Diffring took time off from playing all those blonde Nazi villains in British war movies to be the Venusian who had come to earth to 'Spread a little Love' which turned out to be the title of one of several highly forgettable songs. Paddy and Irving did, however, contribute some well-crafted numbers.

Did I want to be a pop star? Mr Newell dashed backstage after the opening night apparently stunned by my 'American' stage energy and made the offer. 'I can see your face on posters from coast to coast!' My inability to sing apparently had no bearing on the situation. I turned him down (probably unwisely). This was not as odd as it seems in retrospect; all sorts of youngsters from Tommy Steele and Adam Faith to Billy Fury and Marty Wilde were being discovered in coffee bars and street corners.

We came off at the Prince of Wales to be replaced by Pat Kirkwood in *Chrysanthemum*. There were dark rumours at the time about Ms Kirkwood's alleged relationship with Prince Philip being the reason for coming off early. It was far more likely, however, to have been the sheer ghastliness of the show.

Knowing Paddy and Irving meant I was off and running with television work. This was the heyday of 'light entertainment' and there were series and specials everywhere you looked. They all wanted a portion of a severely limited pot of male dancers. I worked with many choreographers of varying quality, but Paddy and Irving were the class acts of the time. Paddy specialised in near technically impossible contemporary jazz work. He would see some stunning use of props in a Kabuki company or whatever and insist we handle them as well as they did while dancing at speed. Irving was more relaxed and his work was laid back, with nice touches of humour.

Dolores Grey came over from Hollywood to do a television special.

She had made her name here in the original London production of *Annie Get Your Gun* at the Palace. Both Paddy and Irving had been in the production along with Wendy Toye, who was later to have a huge influence on my career. This show, however, was to be Irving's and he contracted me to be one of eight boys supporting Ms Grey. One of the difficulties at this time was that neither the BBC nor the Independent Broadcasters had any permanent rehearsal spaces. Television Centre hadn't even been thought of. The companies rented rooms anywhere they could get hold of all over London.

Getting to the first rehearsal could be problematic, but I arrived bright and early to a filthy Scout Hut built in a railway arch by Vauxhall Station. Not only was the dirt a problem but trains regularly rumbled overhead drowning out the accompanist. The neighbourhood in those days was not the most salubrious either, but none of this seemed to bother Dolores. One of my favourite memories was the sight of our star striding down to the corner greasy spoon café at lunchtimes wearing an inch of slap on her face, incredibly high heels and a floor length mink coat.

Although much of the work was instantly forgettable due to the sheer volume of stuff being churned out, there were a few gold nuggets amongst the dross. One of my real regrets was that all this was before the routine use of videotape. It made for a great rush of excitement doing everything live, but once performed it was lost forever. Two contrasting series stand out. *On the Bright Side*, starring Stanley Baxter and Betty Marsden, revived the art of sophisticated revue. It had very high production values and the director had the licence to spend time and money on quality material. Alfred Rodriguez from the Royal Ballet, for instance, was brought in to choreograph a charming little ballet for me, Una Stubbs and Amanda Barrie. Both ladies went on to pursue highly successful acting careers, but I'd dearly love a recording of them as the sweet young dancing gamines they once were.

The other memorable series was very different. *Cool for Cats* was a teatime precursor of *Top of the Pops*. It ran for several seasons and at one point came on three times a week. It had a resident disc jockey who would introduce the latest records and the original artist would occasionally sing the hit live. I remember a very young and nervous Lulu, for instance. Mainly, however, the record would be played and we would perform choreographed routines inspired by the song. This was the main difference to what was to come later. We never just jigged about improvising; this was hard professional graft. Several choreographers were used during its run, but the last series that I did was for Peter Darrell. Peter was later to take over the Scottish Ballet and make it a run-away success, but in those days he was just scratching around making a living like all of us, taking whatever work came along.

Cool for Cats was hardly high art, but when the very last show was announced Peter decided to go out with a bang. Mel Tormé had released a nine-minute version of the classic 'Blues in the Night' and Mr Darrell decided to make it into a tragic modern ballet. He devised a rudimentary plot involving our hero (guess who) being torn between the love of a good woman and a glamorous night-club hostess and eventually coming to a sticky end. It began with me lying in a seedy hotel bedroom smoking a cigarette while a neon light outside blinked on and off through the slats of a venetian blind. (Very atmospheric, but I bet they wouldn't allow the ciggie nowadays.) It moved back and forth through several sets showing domestic bliss contrasted with my frenetic nightlife. Remember this is all live, so costume changes were done on the run between sets. They set up a camera outside the studio at the corner of the building for the grisly climax. I, for plot reasons I can't remember, ran down the road towards the camera on one side of the studio, chased by the rest of the cast, while a car sped towards it from the right angle on the other side.

At a certain climactic note of music, the car and I met in front of the camera, I crashed against the bonnet, fell 'spectacularly' as requested and rolled to my mark in the road. Meanwhile the car driver applied the brakes and stopped on his mark a few inches away from my head. The camera swung up to show the two women in my life united in grief while the props man threw some blood around me for the final shot of me paying for my life of pleasure. I MUST HAVE BEEN MAD!!!

Wouldn't it be heaven to have a recording of that little lot? Most of the other tellies in that first year were more civilised. I did a *Chelsea at Nine* introducing a skinny kid from Tiger Bay called Shirley Bassey. I did the *A to Z* series with the television pundit Alan Melville. I worked on my first film, a truly awful Norman Wisdom picture called *Follow a Star*. Things were going fine, but then it was announced that *West Side*

My Spotlight *photograph (the actor's directory).*

Story was coming over from Broadway. Although I had no real interest in the show initially, this production was to change the course of my life.

Chapter 7

Persuaded into West Side…*thrown on as Riff…Chita Rivera and
the on-stage rape…six weeks of twenty-hour working days…a son
is born*

I HAD HEARD ABOUT the extraordinary impact *West Side Story* had
when it exploded on Broadway and everyone over here was buzzing
with excitement when it was announced that it would be opening in the
West End. Everyone but me, that is. I was totally convinced that I
couldn't possibly appear in it. Wasn't this exactly the sort of modern
American dancing that Jerome Robbins had been creating for American
Ballet Theatre and that I was 'far too classically trained' to cope with?

I was looking forward to seeing it, but I ignored the replacement
auditions and quietly went about the far less stressful business of being
run over on live television. What I hadn't realised was that the
American company opening here had two major problems. Firstly, there
was a sort of running visa situation where the first company member
had to be replaced within three months with others following as the
months ticked away. Secondly, because Robbins had so successfully
instilled The Method into a group of young inexperienced, if highly
talented actor/dancers, the injury rate was horrendous. There were
always several more bodies littering the stage at the end of the first act
rumble than the script actually specified.

The casting director for H. M. Tennants, the company who were
bringing it into Her Majesty's, started ringing Peg at home as soon as it
opened. Wouldn't Paddy care to just come in and talk over possibilities?
Would a little higher salary than normal be of interest? etc. This went
on for days and as I was filming out at Pinewood, I was unavailable and
could carry on ignoring the whole situation. Oh, the bliss of life before
mobile phones!

In the end I gave in and went to dance and read for Peter Gennaro,
Robbins' assistant choreographer. I agreed to the dance audition mainly

to convince myself that I could actually do justice to the style and decided to read to show them I could play it. I'd seen the production by this time and along with the rest of the country was knocked back in my seat by the incredible power of the piece. Although I still played hard to get, I was desperate to be part of what was obviously destined to become part of Musical Theatre history.

I was offered the part of Big Deal, one of the Jets, and agreed on condition that I understudied Riff, the leader of the gang. One of the odd facts about the original production that needs explaining to those brought up on the film version is that Riff was played over here by George Chakiris, who ended up playing the opposing gang leader, Bernardo, in the movie. So George, despite the heavy brown make-up in the picture, was at heart the all-American boy. I was his same height and build and was primed to replace him when necessary.

The problem was that I had only begun the process when all hell broke loose. The company manager called me two weeks after I'd joined the company to say that George had twisted his ankle on the way to the theatre and that I was on that night as Riff. Oh, boy! Now then, I'd had two dance rehearsals where I'd blocked the opening skirmishes and learned the Dance Hall routine. I'd had one walk-through of the lines and moves with the stage manager. I'd had one go around the piano of the two solo songs, but hadn't got as far as the intricate quintet and, more crucially, I'd never rehearsed the knife fight.

There was no time for any proper rehearsal. If I'd started with one scene, it would just panic the rest. I met everyone on stage at the half-hour call. Laurence Leonard, the conductor, was wonderful. He pointed out that he had twenty-two of the best musicians in London in the pit. I was not to try to pick out the opening note of the Jet Song from the tricky Leonard Bernstein underscoring of my dialogue. 'Hit any key you like, I'll take out anything that clashes with you and we'll drift straight back with you.' Whether such a thing was possible or not didn't matter, it gave me confidence. Dear Mr Leonard, he later took over the Hallé orchestra and was eventually knighted.

Ken Le Roy, the original Broadway Bernardo, must have been desperately worried about having to do the knife fight unrehearsed. He knew, however, that I'd had two weeks of watching onstage as Big Deal and so knew the mechanics of when things should happen. He too remained calm and just advised me to relax as much as possible on the throws and falls and with luck we'd both avoid serious injury. All the other 'grown-up' professionals like Chita Rivera were similarly supportive. I then looked round for my gang, The Jets, to find them having a meeting as to whether they could win the rumble that night with a new leader!! I mean there's a time and a place for method acting but it didn't strike me that this was it.

It happened too quickly that first time for me to grasp the full significance of the situation. This was very early in the run of a hugely successful musical and I was to be thrown on, unrehearsed, to play with the highly acclaimed original cast. Peg knew; she sat at home rigid with terror, hiding under the duvet. I just climbed into George's jeans and t-shirt, got through the opening encounters with no disasters and then made my way to the prompt corner to join Don McKay as Tony for the persuasion scene in front of the drug store. As we waited for our entrance, Tony Chardet, the company manager, peered over my shoulder and cheerfully remarked, 'Oh, look, there's Judy Garland sitting front row centre.' I could just as cheerfully have throttled him.

Modesty insists I cast a veil over the success or otherwise of that memorable evening…Oh, what the hell…Kenny Le Roy came to my dressing room afterwards saying, 'It was the most exciting night since the opening on Broadway.' He was probably just thankful we had both survived the knife fight unscathed. What did happen that night and what I used to judge my many later performances in the role was the scream from the audience when I ran on to the knife at the climax of the fight. If you didn't get that startled shriek something had gone wrong with your timing.

George recovered and we settled into what was to be the first of my many long runs in the West End. I got to be a sort of totem. Everything I did ran for at least eighteen months or more. A lot of nonsense is talked about the difficulties of keeping a performance fresh in an extended run. The whole point about live theatre is that it is just that, live. Anything can happen and usually does. You can be far more bored after running for two weeks than after two years. In the middle of the run it was announced that George was off to Hollywood to make the film version and that I would take over Riff for the anticipated eight weeks' shooting. Luckily for me, it dragged on for nine months.

I've already mentioned Chita's performance. I would watch her perform 'America' every night from the wings. She had a back like a whiplash and that wonderful throaty powerful voice. A simply exceptional artist. She was involved in what were probably my worst few minutes on stage ever. I was playing Riff one hot and sultry matinée. This was long before air-conditioning. We got to the drug store scene where Chita, as Anita, comes unwillingly to deliver a message from her sister, Maria, to the hero, Tony. She is taunted by the Jets instead and thrown to the ground and the youngest member of the gang, Baby John, is lowered on to her. This is then broken up by Doc, the drugstore owner, bursting in. Unfortunately, David Bauer had fallen asleep in his dressing room three floors up. For the time it took for an Assistant Stage Manager to race up the stairs, wake David, drag him downstairs and throw him on, we had nothing to do on stage except to carry on raping Chita. The brass had an eight bar repeat at that point that pounded on and on and on. The boys hadn't the experience to override their methodology and do anything else other than to continue raping.

Chita was becoming hysterical, her clothes were being ripped and the situation was getting out of hand. I tried to pull them off shouting 'She's not worth it' and stuff like that but it was a close run thing. When relief finally arrived Chita pulled herself up with her make-up streaked over her face, held her torn dress together, and delivered her parting line with such venom that we were all shattered.

Normally the show ran without such high drama, but the tension backstage was palpable. The two gangs dressed on either side of the theatre and were encouraged by Jerry Robbins never to speak or socialise with each other. The British replacements gradually diffused the over intense atmosphere but after two years I'd had enough. The show was to go out on tour but I'd heard about a new American musical about to open called *How to Succeed in Business without Really Trying* that sounded more cheerful.

Meanwhile I'd worked on the first Cliff Richard picture, *The Young Ones*, and done a season of cabaret at The Embassy Club in Mayfair while playing Riff at the same time. This meant a six-week overlap of working from seven in the morning to three o'clock the following morning. Luckily Riff only appears in the Dream Ballet in the second act after being killed, so I could grab a nap before the curtain calls.

The big news, however, was that our son, Patrick Gair, was born on 28 November 1959. I always place when *West Side* happened in my life by the age of my son. It's hard to believe he's nearly forty-three!

Chapter 8

*The domestic front…a temperate climate…houses and food…our
first car…we move down to Kent*

LIFE ON THE domestic front was proceeding at its own rhythm.
Getting used to living in a strange country, rather than just visiting
or touring, kept throwing up surprises. The temperate climate for
instance. Having arrived in September, I was unconsciously waiting for
the grass to turn brown and the snows to come. When the lawns stayed
a lush green all year round, I was astonished. One Sunday in our first
February over here the temperature was an unseasonable 65°F and we
decided on a picnic in Richmond Park. As we lolled about on a blanket
under the trees and watched the herds of deer peacefully grazing nearby,
I remembered the Februaries of my childhood when you negotiated
your way to school through six-foot snowdrifts.

This was a new world. I was agog, the children were coping well, and
Peg, of course, was in her element. We'd been sent initially to an
adequate, if not very exciting, apartment in Sandycombe Road, which
was in the area of, but not actually on, Kew Green. Within a few weeks
Peg discovered a pretty little Victorian end-of-terrace cottage facing the
duck pond on the Green for the same rent, the grand sum of £7 a week.
It was a lovely little place: two up, two down with a charming spiral
staircase leading from the master bedroom to the loft room. There was
a problem, however; Peg was pregnant and as soon as the baby needed a
room of its own, the dear little house would be just too small.

Meanwhile there was the food to get used to. Rationing had finished,
but the supplies of produce were still very limited. As has been
mentioned, Peg could, and did, work miracles, but her forte was the
main dish; she didn't have my sweet tooth. I took to dreaming about
luscious deep fruit pies, lemon pies with three inches of meringue on
top, pecan and Black Bottom, Angel Food and Devil's Food cakes. THE
VICTORIA SPONGE IS NOT THE SAME! In desperation I got my

sister to ship over a proper ten-inch diameter, four-inch high Angel Cake tin and I taught myself to be a pastry chef! Having just sat down from preparing an Orange/Chocolate chiffon cake for a friend's 83rd birthday, I'm pleased to say that the old hands have not lost their cunning.

Then, of course, there was driving. I'd never driven in Canada, so the 'wrong' side of the road was not a real problem. What could have been, however, was the speed of having to learn. What with the added expense of the baby and all, I signed for a six-month contract at the Embassy Club on Bond Street in Mayfair. I thought, in my innocence, that the tubes ran all night. I was wrong. There was no way of getting back to Kew after the second show at two in the morning. I therefore took myself down to the local used-car dealer and bought a 1936 black Standard automobile for £15.

I loved that car. It looked like all the gangster movies of the thirties. It had a divided front windscreen and, in its sloping back, two little triangular rear windows. The kindly used-car dealer gave me a lesson and I launched myself into the world. I spent the next six months making my way up to the centre of London every night and back again to Kew in the early morning without anything as mundane as tax or insurance. In those days Eros was still in the centre of Piccadilly Circus and I remember the first time driving round and round him under the bemused gaze of a traffic policeman, until I got enough courage to move to the right lane to exit. Neither he nor any other policeman ever stopped me in my travels.

It was very noisy at first until someone told me you had to double de-clutch and showed me how. We used to go on family expeditions as well. By that time, someone else had told me that you had to put water in the radiator, so having rested halfway up Box Hill and topped up, we arrived in style on top to admire the extraordinary view.

In those days, Mayfair was very, very grand. Even the Ladies of the Night who waved you a cheery goodnight after you came out from a late show tended to have posh accents. The automobile agencies only sold Rolls-Royce and Bentleys (come to think of it, they still do) and their garages had smartly uniformed young men to attend to you. The concept of self-service was a long way off. On one occasion the long-suffering family had joined me in Bond Street to drive home after a rehearsal. I needed petrol so I stopped in one of these emporiums. I pulled up at the pumps, the young man approached and stood smartly awaiting instructions. I rolled down the window and it went right through the rust on the bottom of the door to land at his feet. I went a trifle red, Peg collapsed in sadistic laughter while the poor children in the back seat died of mortification. The young man, with merely a hint of a raised left eyebrow, picked up the window and politely handed it back to me through the empty frame.

Having finished its six months' duty, the plucky Standard was finally falling apart. In the end I sold it back to the original seller for £5 for scrap and was quite content. I moved on to newer and slightly more respectable cars (and passed my driving test first time) but nothing will ever replace that first love.

When Patrick Gair's birth became imminent, Peg developed some slight complications and it was decided she would spend the last few days in Windsor hospital. The question of me being in on the birth never arose because women of Peg's generation regarded birth as a female ceremony and the last thing they wanted was a spare man cluttering up the place. I was still in *West Side* and we'd taken to doing excerpts in various shows for charity. We'd already been asked to do 'Cool' for Margot Fonteyn at her annual Royal Academy of Dance Matinée. This time it was a midnight matinée at Drury Lane for Prince Philip. I'd been told that the baby was due in a few days so it took a while to make sense of my telephone call the following morning. On enquiring about how my wife was doing, the reply was 'Oh, they're doing fine.'

My first sight of the new arrival was when the nurse held him up for me to peer through the glass. Because he'd been born with fingernails, they'd tied little white cotton mittens on him to avoid scratches. He looked like a miniature Rocky Marciano. Back home in Kew life settled down with the children in local schools, me commuting into work on the District Line and Peg walking the pram around the stunning Kew Gardens. We decided when the time came to move on that we'd have to go out into the country to get more room for the same money. The freeholder of our little cottage was anxious to sell and offered it to us for £3,000, but we couldn't possibly afford that amount of money. Now, of course, it's worth seven figures. C'est la vie.

What we found was half of an enormous redbrick Queen Anne pile deep in the Kent countryside. It was a substantial manor house that had been sold and rather arbitrarily split down the middle. One half had the extensive grounds and four bedrooms, but we had the rose garden to the front and a huge vegetable patch to the rear, the two great drawing rooms on the ground and first floors and eight, count 'em, eight bedrooms. Oh, and not a stick of furniture. All of this for the same rent, £7 a week! We were offered a seven, fourteen, or twenty-one-year lease and opted (foolishly) for the shortest. It worked out well as we bought our first house after seven years, but to think we could have been paying that peppercorn rent into the 1980s!

Peg saw a competition in the *Daily Telegraph* offering a complete kitchen for an essay about one's ideal version and set about winning that. The rest we bought at auction. There was a monthly auction in Sevenoaks that we attended religiously. Because everyone in the 1960s was after small furniture and light wood, we could pick up enormous beautiful mahogany stuff that wouldn't even get in the door of the flats of the time. I got a huge beautiful many-drawered chest for £11, for instance, and the deliverymen offered me £14 for the brass handles alone.

So began a thirty-year commute into the West End from the country that I actually found less tiring than the vagaries of the District Line. It also started a deep love of Kent. The first evening we went for a little drive through the tiny lanes that were to become so familiar to us. Suddenly I saw a man striding along above the height of the hedge to one side of the road. I thought I was hallucinating until we came to a gap. He was walking on stilts to string his hop poles. They still grow an enormous amount of hops for beer making in Kent, but I bet a fancy machine has replaced that man working away at the top of his poles with such quiet efficiency.

Chapter 9

The Young Ones, Nora Kaye and Herbert Ross…the Embassy Club…magicians and strippers…How to Succeed in Business…Frank Loessor and Billy de Wolfe…the ITV strike… taken to court

THE INTERESTING THING about doing the first Cliff Richard picture *The Young Ones* from my point of view was that the American, Herbert Ross, choreographed it. Herbie went on to become a distinguished Hollywood director, but I'd worked for him before when he had come to American Ballet Theatre to do a quite dazzlingly pretentious bit of codswallop for Nora Kaye called, I believe, *Winter's Eve*. It was all about Nora being a poor blind girl and we were all birds who lifted her and made her fly to make up for her loss of sight. Johnny Kriza played her boyfriend and for some reason we pecked out his eyes as well, leaving them to tap, tap, tap across the stage trying to find each other.

Herbie seemed a highly unlikely choice to stage an English pop singer's first picture, but he did a nice job and it stands up pretty well even now. I quite like the Mambo that four of us do with the leading lady in black suits, bowler hats and umbrellas on a shiny red floor. The point is that he and Nora were now married and, to make the trip more viable, she was on the payroll as his assistant. She became a 'gopher' on the picture and worked conscientiously with no sense of regretting her loss of status, but I felt it was almost sacrilegious to have this great ballerina mop one's brow after a take with a cologne-soaked chamois leather.

When they came back the next year to do *Summer Holiday*, Herbie asked me to be in that one as well, but though I'd managed to combine *West Side Story* with the first picture, I couldn't get away from my then current theatre contract to do all the location shooting required for this one. I was persuaded to sign the contract anyway and eventually appeared for about thirty seconds in a barn scene they shot in London. At least I'm told I appear; I've never actually been able to spot myself. I'll return later to my valuable treatise on how to make a lot of money from the movies by appearing as little as possible.

The Embassy Club cabaret run was an enlightening experience. There were five of us, three female and two male, who provided the opening and finale numbers plus filling in between the visiting acts that changed every week. There were magicians and strippers and all sorts of novelty acts. There were only two dressing-rooms, one at the side and the other above the tiny stage. Depending on the requirements of the visitors, we fitted in where we could. The only really tiresome week was sharing a minute room with a magician whose entire act consisted of gradually producing hundreds and hundreds of doves concealed about his person. It was fine once they were all folded into his costume, but he liked to have them flap around to exercise beforehand. I felt like Tippi Hedron in *The Birds*.

My favourite dressing room mate was the stripper, Marquise. She was a lovely lady, very charming and funny. She was also a very fine dancer whose two numbers included a take on the Sally Rand strip, where layers of fine chiffon were progressively removed, and a more dramatic fire number. (Sally Rand was an American rival stripper to Gypsy Rose Lee. She danced with layers of veil and as she twirled towards the wings one would drift offstage where unseen hands would remove it. Miss Rand would seem to become naked as if by magic.) I managed to sneak in to see Sally's other speciality, the Fan Dance, when I was about fourteen. She was touring with the Royal American Shows, a giant summer fair and midway* that came round to Winnipeg every year. She danced with two strategically manipulated enormous ostrich feather fans and, as the tension built, climbed a staircase with them behind her. As the drum rolled she turned to the front, threw open her arms and posed for approximately a millisecond before the inevitable blackout. An artiste!

Among our little 'permanent' company at the club was the lovely Lynda Baron. Lynda's another of my former partners to go on to a busy acting career. Back in those days she was incredibly glamorous, with

---

*midway: the sideshows and stalls at a fair.

wonderful long red hair, a tiny waist, super long legs and, of course, a terrific voice. She had a solo singing spot before the finale and wore a silver lamé fishtail dress. It was strapless and skin-tight down to the knees and then blossomed out into a froth of tulle. Very sexy. She wore very high heels and could only totter as her knees were effectively tied together. All went well until she tripped over her mike lead one night. Down she went and, of course, couldn't get up. She floundered about like a beached mermaid. The other chap in the act and I tried to get ourselves more or less under control before staggering on to rescue her. Years later I choreographed *Cinderella* at Bromley and had Lynda as my Prince Charming and Una Stubbs as my heroine. Lovely ladies, happy days.

On to *How to Succeed*. I've been incredibly lucky to work with some real heroes throughout my career and this show supplied several. Frank Loessor was already a legend as the composer of *Guys and Dolls* and both he and the wonderful American humorist, Abe Burrows, came over to cast and rehearse the show. The auditions were exhausting. In dance you had to cope with the hard-edged Broadway bash of the Pirate number as well as the emerging style of the young Bob Fosse. The male singers were still auditioned separately from the male dancers. When the former sang, they could choose whatever audition piece they liked whereas we dancers all had to sing 'Blue Skies.' Once I got to know him better during the rehearsal period I asked Mr Loesser why we had to stick to this one particular number. 'Sibilance,' he replied. 'If you can get through – "blue skies smiling at me, nothing but blue skies do I see" – without sibilance, you can play butch, my son.' Not very politically correct, but effective, I suppose. He then proceeded to hypnotise those of us who had got through to hit and sustain notes that we were convinced were totally out of our range. A real master of his craft.

My other hero on the show was Billy de Wolfe, who played the boss of the company. Billy was pure old style Hollywood gold. Most of those musicals of the forties that I had worshipped as a child had him playing a supporting lead. He had a pencil thin moustache and a slightly fey manner and was very, very funny. In a couple of pictures he did his Mrs Murgatroyd, which he must have brought with him from Vaudeville. It was a sort of American version of Les Dawson's gossipy lady played in a perfectly correct suit and tie but with a dizzy female hat plonked on his head. His other speciality was to do a perfectly straightforward exit but at the last minute kick the back of his head. He'd then pull himself together, purse his lips disapprovingly and go on his way.

We played at the Shaftesbury Theatre that had always had a reputation for bad luck. Nothing seemed to run for very long there. It was on Shaftesbury Avenue but on the wrong side of Cambridge Circus. It seemed to have hit the jackpot with *Hair* but it had to close when plaster from the ceiling fell down onto the balcony. To counteract all these bad vibes our company had it remodelled and changed its name to the Princes Theatre. It seemed to work up to a point, the show had a very respectable run, but there was always a slight feeling that it wasn't quite the smash hit it should have been.

After these big American Broadway shows my next was to be very different. *Robert and Elizabeth*, written by Ronald Millar about the relationship between Elizabeth Barrett and Robert Browning was about as English a project as you could imagine, although both leads, June Bronhill and Keith Michell, were Australian. Directed and choreographed by Wendy Toye, who unbelievably had directed for Cochran in her teens and is still going strong, this was to be a very happy experience. Before starting with the new show, however, I'd been involved with more tellies, including the original *Sunday Night at the London Palladium* with Bruce Forsyth, a year of cabaret at the Talk of the Town, supporting Eartha Kitt amongst others, survived a devastating Equity strike against ITV and been hauled up in court for non-payment of rates. Life was not entirely beer and skittles.

The problem was the Palladium show. It only paid nine guineas. To those who don't remember real money, a guinea is a pound and a shilling, very useful when negotiating contracts. 'Will you accept xxx pounds?' 'Never, make it guineas!'

The job didn't take up much of your time. You learned three numbers on the Friday, worked in the theatre Saturday morning, had camera rehearsals on Sunday and it went out live on Sunday evening. It only worked financially, however, if you could combine it with something else. I signed up for the new season and also accepted a contract at Talk of the Town for £17 a week. Neither was enough to support the family, but together all was well.

After three Palladiums, Equity in its wisdom decided to strike against commercial television, which meant that for six months nothing was on ITV except news and documentaries. I, meanwhile, had to fulfil my cabaret contract without enough money to live on. In my innocence I decided it was more important to keep abreast of the local grocery and butcher bills, etc. and to leave the rates till I started the new job. I was mistaken and found myself appearing in Maidstone Crown Court for non-payment of £50 to the Government.

'Did I need a lawyer?' I asked nervously. 'No, no, no' I was told. I was not to worry but just explain that I had recently started on *Robert and Elizabeth* and would pay it off at £5 per week. My name was called and I stood up to give evidence. The judge asked 'Are you in work?'

'Yes,' I replied.

'What is your weekly salary?'

'£30, your honour.'

At this point the judge went ballistic. He ranted on about people on high salaries trying to cheat the system and rob from their fellow citizens and, without allowing me a word of explanation of the circumstances, demanded the £50 be paid into court that same afternoon or I'd go to gaol! Shock, horror! I phoned dear Nessie Tierney at the Equity office. She was a little Scottish lady who came round the West End theatres every week to collect dues and exchange knitting patterns and such. (It was a much more homely world in those days.) 'Dinna you mind, hen,' she said, 'I'll send someone doon on a bike.' Sure enough, as the deadline approached, a motorcycle roared up with a young chap on board clutching £50 in his hand. I could have kissed him. As a matter of fact I probably did. Deliverance!

Chapter 10

*Robert and Elizabeth…Sir Donald Wolfit…Gillian Lynne and
Half a Sixpence…on to the property ladder*

MARTIN LANDAU, not the stolid American movie actor of the same name, but a rather flamboyant English producer with a reputation for sailing a trifle close to the wind, produced *Robert and Elizabeth*. His main claim to fame before this was the discovery of Audrey Hepburn. He gave her a job as a dancer in one of his early West End revues before she became famous, and dined out on the story for years. He had sound theatrical taste, however, and spent a lot of money producing what he hoped would be the break-through British musical. Ronald Millar, who was later to write many of Mrs Thatcher's more memorable phrases, wrote a literate and sensitive book and Ron Grainer a tuneful lilting score. June Bronhill, the very fine Australian soprano was Elizabeth, and the young Keith Michell a dashing and romantic Browning. What gave the show its gravitas, however, was the casting of Sir John Clements as Elizabeth's sadistic Papa. It was unheard of in those days for a serious stage actor to appear in a musical.

The elaborate sets included a charming train for the lovers to escape on and ingenious sliding transitions from hall and staircase to bedroom and back again with ease. The sets were made for Her Majesty's Theatre and we set out on tour with this as our destination. Playing there at the time was a small cast courtroom drama that included the redoubtable actress Coral Browne. Here is where events become a trifle murky. The cast of the play were due to sign new contracts. If they didn't, however, the theatre would be available for *Robert and Elizabeth*. Mr Landau allegedly decided to ensure this eventuality by attempting to offer them bribes to cut and run. Ms Browne took umbrage at this and decided to spill the beans. Threats of court actions for real! The upshot was the show had to come into town to the smaller Lyric Theatre on Shaftesbury Avenue. Three feet had to be rudely cut from the width of the beautiful sets, but more crucially, the theatre was just too small for the show ever to make money. It could be a big hit, (it was), it could run and run, (it did), but did it make Martin a fortune? 'Not bloody likely,' to quote Eliza Doolitle.

Still, it was a nice little earner for yours truly, particularly when the film of *Half a Sixpence* came along during the second year of its run and I managed to combine both at once. Before this, however, Sir John had been replaced by another theatrical knight, Sir Donald Wolfit. In the production, as in real life, Elizabeth had eight brothers. I was earning my extra bits of cash by understudying most of them and, as such, came in for Sir Donald's rehearsals to block him into the show. He learned the role and his moves and only insisted on minor changes, mainly due to paranoia about his lack of height. Where Clements would stand at stage level, Sir Donald would stand on the first stair or on the fireplace guard – that sort of thing.

He was grateful to the few of us that had worked him through all this and, once he'd opened, took us to the Garrick Club (the famous theatrical gathering hole) for lunch. He was a wonderful raconteur and told us all sorts of stories about his early years touring in England and America. One particular anecdote concerned his playing *Oedipus Rex* on a tour of the States. Sir Donald was very much an actor/manager of the old school and was particularly proud of his extraordinary and powerful voice, which was immortalised when Albert Finney, playing the fictionalised version of him in the film *The Dresser*, stopped the train at Crewe station. Sir Donald used this huge instrument to great effect in the climactic moment of the play when his eyes are plucked out off-stage. He would produce a terrible blood-curdling animal shriek before coming back on stage with stage blood pouring down his face.

In one particular venue, a converted school auditorium with very dark wings, he came off stage, grabbed hold of the nearest pillar for support, took a deep breath and bellowed the famous drawn-out scream. On this occasion, however, the black pillar collapsed at his feet in a dead faint. It turned out to be the statutory fireman on duty, an impressive six-foot five-inch stalwart, but who had never been back stage before in his life. I asked Sir Donald, 'What did you do?'

'Well,' he said nonchalantly, 'I stepped over the body, applied my

With Tommy Steele and Neil Fitzwilliam in the film of Half a Sixpence.

blood, and went back on stage.' History does not relate the fate of the traumatised fire fighter.

Although I had made several films previously, the two Cliff Richard ones, a forgettable Norman Wisdom vehicle called *Follow a Star* and a truly horrendous effort called *Pop Gear* which involved a lot of gyrating around in the then currently fashionable bum-freezer Italian suits, *Half a Sixpence* in 1965 set the pattern for a series of very profitable ventures for me and my fellow dancers. For the next decade or so Hollywood decided that it was cheaper to make the big blockbusting musicals over here in England and several of us went from one to another until it became practically like going in to the office.

The pattern of employment was the same for each movie. Sixteen dancers, eight male, eight female, would be signed for 'run of the picture' contracts. We were called the skeleton crew. As the film progressed, other dancers would be added to flesh out the big numbers as they came up, but we stayed on salary from start to finish. As the films in those days took anything from six months to a year to make, this was obviously a good deal. This was particularly apparent later when Mark Breaux and Dee Dee Wood came over from Hollywood to audition us for *Chitty Chitty Bang Bang*. They were fresh from their success in choreographing *Mary Poppins* and wanted to ensure they got the best dancers before *Oliver!* snapped them up for the same time frame. Their problem was that the shooting script hadn't been finished, so our run of the picture contract eventually amounted to two weeks' work at the beginning of shooting, the same at the end, and six months of sitting at home collecting our weekly cheque. Heaven!

The business of how often one appeared on screen was governed by the nature of the film, whether it was contemporary or period and how much time passed in the story. If the plot followed someone's life, it's obvious that the same face remaining the same age would look farcical if it kept popping up while the hero aged. You either managed to appear slightly out of focus in the background of each number or adopted elaborate disguises. The ludicrous *Song of Norway* (of which more later) took the latter approach. They togged me out in different shades of wigs, beards and moustaches for each successive number and I ended up looking either like Che Guevara or Shirley Temple.

Back to *Half a Sixpence*. This was my first encounter with both Tommy Steele and the choreographer Gillian Lynne. Tommy was on a steep upward curve to stardom. In a sense he was too successful in the role for the good of the film. The Hollywood moguls insisted that the daily rushes were sent over and became more and more excited about the possibilities. What started out as a charming little musical picture became more and more overblown. More numbers were added and production values soared. It managed to retain most of its charm, but lost a lot of pace along the way.

I spent a lot of years working with Gillian Lynne after that first encounter either as her assistant or just appearing in her stage or television productions. She had a long and painful struggle doing distinguished but not particularly lucrative work before hitting the

Between takes.

jackpot firstly with *Cats* and then quickly following with *Phantom of the Opera*. No one deserved it more.

Much as I enjoyed working with Gillie and Tommy on the picture and having the stability of the long West End run, the real personal significance of combining those two jobs was being able to amass a down payment for our first house. We were on the property ladder just like real people! Outside a village down in deepest Kent called Ightham (think of Night-ham or Right-ham, not Igg-tham) there is a wooded hill called Oldbury. It has the remains of an ancient pre-historic hill fort on its flat top, a Roman road winding up it and its woods are covered in bluebells in May. On its lower slopes in the 1930s a speculator built two short rows of semi-detached houses before being thwarted (thank goodness) by the National Trust acquiring the hill. We bought the end semi on the Upper road. It was a perfectly ordinary little Thirties three-bedroom house but built in this extraordinary location. It had a long and beautiful (after Peg got to work on it) garden with a private gate leading into the acres of National Trust woods and paths leading up the hill. We settled down there to twenty-six years of domestic bliss. By coincidence it was the same price as the house had been on Kew Green, £3,000. To the end of her life dear Peg insisted that I'd got a decimal point wrong when I tried to explain to her that we eventually sold it for £130,000.

Chapter 11

Family life in the village…Polari in the dressing room…children
and grandchildren…education and the National Health system

Although Ightham is barely twenty-five miles from London and commutable by fast train from Sevenoaks in half an hour, when we settled there it still retained a good deal of its ancient village values and sense of place and time. Being right in the middle of the Green Belt, it was protected from development and so we were surrounded by orchards and hop fields and, of course, the unspoilt woods and hills. The village blacksmith still hadn't become a garage, and a good many of the locals had never been up to London in their lives. What's more, they saw no good reason to attempt the hazardous journey.

People in 'the business' used to joke about my Jekyll and Hyde existence. They swore that halfway home on the train I threw off the spangles and glitter of show business and donned the tweeds and pipe of the country squire. It's true I did live two quite separate lives in that sense. Maybe it's something to do with being a Gemini, although I have no faith at all in Astrology. I was perfectly happy in both worlds and probably remained sane and balanced because of it. At work, in the high camp atmosphere of a boy dancers' dressing room in a West End show, I could hold my end up in high-powered bitchery and, of course, Polari. 'What is Polari?' you might well ask. Well, it was essentially a secret language distilled from Romany gypsies and circus slang that had been refined and adapted by the more flamboyant homosexuals of the time. Kenneth Williams and Hugh Paddick purloined it for their Jules and Sandy personae in the Radio series *Beyond Our Ken*.

The idea was that one could talk disgracefully with a friend in a straight environment and not be discovered or understood. 'Vada the polone with the naff aunt-nelling groins,' for instance. Vada (look at) the polone (woman) with the naff (tasteless) aunt-nell (to listen or hear) groins (rings) thus (aunt-nelling groins) earrings. Some of it has survived in today's slang. Naff is still around as in Naff Caff for a greasy spoon café and riah is still used for hair occasionally. Some words like that were just used backwards as in ecaf for face. The point about the language and the etiquette of the dressing rooms is that you shared them cheek by jowl with four or five mates for anything up to two years at a time eight times a week. You either threw yourself into their rarefied world or life became a misery. The other point to make is that they were some of the funniest people you would ever be likely to encounter. Whether the incessant humour covered a darker melancholy is open to question. Homosexuality was after all still an imprisonable offence at the time. Tragedies did occur. One of my friends in the *Robert and Elizabeth* dressing room committed suicide when his partner of fourteen years died and the 'in-laws' who had always been previously supportive discovered they could throw him out of the house they had shared.

Once home in the village, of course, life was very different. Peg had been drawn unwillingly into directing for the local amateur dramatic society. Indeed, she was positively blackmailed into her first one when our local family doctor threatened to withhold treatment unless he could get to play the lead in *Devil's Disciple*. A slight exaggeration? Possibly. She did remain firm, however, in only doing projects that interested her. She never churned out the potboilers and staple fodder of the am-dram circuit. She did a fine modern dress *Midsummer Night's Dream* and David, who is a language scholar, translated a much funnier version of the Feydeau farce *Occupe toi d'Amélie* than Noel Coward's version, *Look after Lulu*. For once The Master stumbled and the play died in the West End. My stepson's version, however, was a hit for the Wrotham Players! Peg also directed a remarkably moving version of the York Mystery plays at the local church. Being totally non-religious, she nevertheless had a profound regard for the King James Version of the Bible and its astonishingly beautiful use of the English language.

All this activity drew her naturally into the centre of village life and I tagged along doing a bit of choreography or whatever when needed. We developed a wide and disparate circle of friends and my sort of dinner party anecdotes resembled reports of a faraway land from a foreign correspondent. There was some crossover, however. Friends came down to stay, occasionally to recuperate when a knee cartilage went (a fairly common occurrence amongst dancers) or once when a wife and child needed refuge from an abusive husband. This latter visit came complete with a large and beautiful Afghan hound. We were still in the big house at the time and our startled neighbour came round on their first morning to report that she'd looked up from her morning coffee to see Veronica Lake on her hands and knees peering in through the patio doors!

The children were blooming. Patrick was just starting in primary school when we bought the house. It was, of course, the perfect place to spend a childhood. The school was down a snickety path by a field with no roads to cross. The hill behind gave endless possibilities for exploring, and for a sports mad child life was an endless round of football and cricket. Ah, cricket! For me as a North American to have grown to love this daft and infuriating game is, I consider, one of my more notable achievements.

David was the brain of the family. When we moved down to Kent we enrolled him in the highly regarded Maidstone Grammar School. After a few weeks the school announced that it would groom him for an Open Scholarship to Oxford. As we had only a vague idea of what this meant, we nodded sagely and waited for events. Sure enough, the years went by and he duly won the Open. He went up to study Modern Languages at Wadham College in Oxford and the Scholarship took care of everything. He must be one of the few university students ever to come home between terms having saved money on his grant!

Hilary had a more difficult time through her teens. She felt isolated down in the country and, being older when we came over, missed the easy camaraderie of her peers in Canada. It also took her a long time to realize that her innate common sense was, if anything, even more valuable in life than the heights of academia. She married a local lad and quickly produced my first two step-grandchildren. The odd side effect of this was that as there are only nine years' difference between Hilary and myself, she has always called me Paddy and our relationship, though close, has not in any sense been father/daughter. With her children, Trant and Emma, however, the generation gap is enough to ensure that from the beginning I have been their 'real' grandfather. This led to some rather odd looks in supermarkets when I'd be followed by toddlers shouting 'Grandad, grandad' when I was still in my early thirties.

David married later in life and produced his two, Thomas and Kitty, and finally Patrick Gair married and had Patrick James and Alice. I now, therefore, have a full set of six grandchildren ranging across the generations. The eldest is thirty-three and the youngest eight. Neat, huh?

None of my children grew up to follow me into the business, although David did have a brief flirtation with stage and company management after coming down from university. Instead of (or perhaps because of) my fly-by-night existence in the 'glamour' world of show biz, they all opted for the security of careers in the law or the Civil Service. Peg and I were delighted, of course, if a trifle puzzled by this universal conformity. This is not to say that they couldn't occasionally surprise one. Patrick Gair worked for me front-of-house for a time early on at the Old Vic. As most FOH staff are aspiring thespians making some extra cash while 'resting', it was natural that they should provide an alternative cabaret for the first anniversary party. The performance standard was generally high, but when my son was announced I had no idea what to expect. Some time before, we had had a worthy, if rather stolid and very long production of *Great Expectations* play the theatre. Patrick announced that he would perform the piece in two and a half minutes flat! This he proceeded to do to devastating effect. Every character, every telling line, every twist of plot was whizzed through in no time at all. It was sharp, accurate and very, very funny. To this day I use 'What larks, Pip' in a Mommerset accent as a catch-all catch-phrase.

Having implicitly endorsed the education system of this remarkable country, in that I never paid a penny towards any child's schooling, I'd better mention my appreciation of the National Health system as well. Although my memories of those sunny years down in Kent are overwhelmingly happy, there were the occasional serious crises. In David's gap year before university, he developed a tumour in the pituitary gland, a millimetre away from the optic nerve. He was operated on up in Perth in Scotland by the leading specialist of the time, who removed the tumour while saving his sight. Not a penny. Hilary had to have an ovary removed. Despite waking up in a ward filled with ghastly old ladies who assured her that she would in future be 'a vegetable, dear, just a vegetable', she not only proved them wrong by

Most of the family; clockwise David, his wife Gillian, Peg, our son Patrick Gair,
Peg's brother Trant, Hilary, me and grandson Trant.

producing her two babies, but had them, as did all the others, for free on the National Health.

Peg's eventual decline once the shadow of Parkinson's fell was far in the future. When it arrived, the distress involved was deep and prolonged, but I can't imagine how much worse it would have been if one had to pay for the pills and treatment involved. Thankfully, foreknowledge is denied us and we had a quarter of a century more of this unusual, (possibly) but happy and satisfying, (definitely) life together.

Chapter 12

*Show-biz rules…*Great Waltz *at Drury Lane…playing two roles at once…stage version of* Gone With the Wind*…back to Hollywood…dying in the horseshit*

I'VE NEVER BEEN ambitious in the usual show-biz sense. The idea of losing one's private life in exchange for being photographed at an endless round of ghastly 'celebrity' parties makes one's flesh crawl. All I've ever wanted was the opportunity to perform and to make a living, a comfortable living if possible, from the crazy business I fell in love with as a child.

Once I'd recognised my worth to the West End, for instance, and to put it crudely, realized how to negotiate my assets, I set about making it happen.

Rules

1. Make yourself as technically adept as possible, i.e. be versatile (or learn to fake it)
2. Make yourself indispensable to the production, i.e. understudy everybody in sight
3. Assist the choreographer
4. Assist the director
5. Sack your agent – it's ludicrous to pay an agent 15 per cent of your weekly salary for two years in return for one telephone call confirming the original audition!
6. Accept whatever comes along. Never hold out for that starring role. It's all work, baby!

I probably wouldn't have been so bold in negotiations if I hadn't had the family to support all those years. Once embarked on this course, however, the tactics stood me in good stead. The plan nearly came to grief, however, when I did *The Great Waltz* at the Theatre Royal, Drury

Lane. The show told (soppily) the life story of Johann Strauss Jr. I understudied Franz, who was the seventeen-year-old (in the plot) principal dancer of the show, as well as the elderly second banana,* who was over from America playing Strauss's manager. When he went home to the States, I took over the role for nine weeks, playing the 65-year old character part (I was in my mid-thirties at the time). Luckily, Drury Lane is a far from intimate venue, so you can get away with playing in fairly broad-brush strokes. It was a lovely part. It had one sure-fire audience-pleasing cross-over where you come on from one side of the stage convulsed in hysterical laughter, make your way to centre stage and try to explain to the dear, late Robert Dorning, playing the owner of the café in the show, that the first comic has been blown up by fireworks off-stage. Not being able to get the story out despite desperate body language, you go off the other side still hysterical, to a nice round of applause.

During my stint as the old man, I was watching on stage when the Radetzky March started. The young Franz was borne in shoulder high by the other dancers. Unfortunately, they put him down badly; he sprained his ankle and limped off stage. Deanne Horsham from the Royal Ballet was panicking, wondering how she was going to perform the number with no partner and, as I was his understudy as well, I – without thinking at all – stepped in and did it, but as the old man, in character. This meant whispering to Deanne as we danced, 'We won't do the big shoulder-high lift, I'll just whirl you around at waist-height' etc. plus a lot of jolly on-the-spot improvising from both of us. It worked, we got clean away with it and that was that. Harold Fielding, the producer, even gave me a £10 bonus for saving the show!

At the end of my nine weeks, Peter Graves joined the cast as contracted (he'd been working elsewhere until then) and I sloped back to the chorus. It can be hard to let go when you've had fun with a part. Lord Graves was a charming, gentle actor and the right age for the role, but come close and I'll whisper, 'He didn't get the exit round I did.'

When the production was about to close, Onna White came over to audition dancers for the remake of the film version of *The Great Waltz*. I got the job and signed my contract. I was pleased because there was

---

*banana: comic actor.

to be some nice location work in Vienna. Harold Fielding, the producer, had other plans. He decided that he liked having the beautiful Drury Lane to produce in and invited the up-and-coming American choreographer/director, Joe Layton, to bring in his lavish musical version of *Gone with the Wind*. For some reason that I've yet to fathom, he decided he wanted me to be in it as well and bought out my contract for the film. I was both flattered (it sounded very glamorous to have your contract bought out) and irritated that he didn't ask me first. At the same time Wendy Toye came to see me and asked me to do an intimate revue she was putting together called *Cowardy Custard* for the Mermaid Theatre. Based on Sir Noel's works, this small cast affair would have a much bigger personal impact than being lost in the burning of Atlanta.

Using my tried and trusted system of just accepting whatever came next (Rule 6), however, I just shrugged my shoulders and got on with rehearsing the monster musical. Joe had previously presented it in an enormous theatre in Tokyo, famous for its effects. It had three stages, each the size of Drury Lane's, joined together in a shallow arc. This had huge advantages, literally, when you're planning to restage the American Civil War, burn down Atlanta, have a train arrive carrying the wounded only for the station to collapse around it, as well as having Scarlett, Melanie and the baby escape at the end of the first act courtesy of a real horse and cart. Oh, brother!

It was amazing watching the mammoth enterprise being put together and to see the vast Drury Lane stage return to its roots as a house of spectacle. A great deal of the show was extremely effective, particularly the train pulling in to the station and the staging of the great Atlanta fire. The first act ended with rows and rows of Spanish moss descending in the mist after the aforementioned escape by Scarlett, who led the horse and cart round the stage from upstage right down to centre front. There was plenty of room for accident and misadventure, and there was plenty of both during the run, but we opened the show with high hopes.

The stunning June Ritchie played Scarlett enchantingly and they brought over the American film star, Harve Presnell, to tackle Rhett Butler. He had played opposite Debbie Reynolds in *The Unsinkable Mollie Brown*. Unfortunately, his playing of the Clark Gable role provoked a London critic to remark: 'His performance was so wooden it's a wonder he didn't go up in flames along with Atlanta.' The six-year-old Bonnie Langford appropriately played their daughter Bonnie in the play. On the opening night everything went well until the horse got over excited and dumped a large and steaming contribution downstage left, while the luckless June was trying to deliver her first act finale number. This, in turn, prompted Sir Noel Coward, sitting out front, to remark later at the opening night party in his clipped but carrying tones, 'If they'd stuffed the child up the horse's arse they'd have had a hit!'

Despite Sir Noel's misgivings, the show settled down and ran for eighteen months. As it came to a close, the Los Angeles Light Opera Society expressed an interest in staging it over there. Fielding then came up with a scheme to stage it for six weeks in LA and then follow it up with a trans-American tour. Joe Layton asked me to come over and help restage the production and then look after it on tour. It really was too good an offer to turn down so once more I packed my bags and hit the road.

The American experience verged on the surreal. For one thing my apartment in Hollywood looked exactly like a set for a mid-budget movie of the period. It was on Franklin, a block from Hollywood Boulevard behind the Chinese Theatre. It was a studio apartment in a white *U*-shaped building built around a swimming pool. You expected a Raymond Chandler character to knock on your door any minute. Competition for jobs in the industry is so much more intense over there that Joe had auditioned 3,000 applicants for the chorus alone. The successful candidates were of a staggeringly high standard and teaching them the choreography was child's play.

The principals were another matter, however. Leslie Ann Warren played Scarlett. She had appeared successfully in a number of movies but seemed physically too tall and brittle for the role. The casting of Rhett compounded the problem. Pernell Roberts had been a huge hit in one of the television cowboy series of the time, but unfortunately was a good two inches shorter than Leslie Ann. Standing on boxes would have worked fine in the movies but this was live on stage and it just looked ludicrous. There were other more serious problems, amongst them the casting of the large and important black cast needed for the play. This was in the mid Seventies and black consciousness quite rightly dictated a serious debate on the seemliness of playing such subservient roles. In the end, the highly distinguished black actors came down on the historical significance of the piece and agreed to carry on.

We rehearsed for four weeks before opening at the Dorothy Chandler Pavilion, the lovely big theatre in LA often used for the Oscars ceremony. The sets had been shipped over from London and looked great. The reviews were passable and we settled down for the agreed six-week run before moving to the Curran Theatre in San Francisco for the same run before setting out on the tour. I had decided that I would hand over all my dancing bits and pieces to an American, but would keep my interest in the thing going by playing the Northern deserter who attempts to rape Scarlett at the end of the first act.

Remember that Spanish moss? Well, when Rhett goes off to join the army and deserts Scarlett, she sinks down in despair by the wagon, and provided the horse hadn't shat that night, has a very poignant moment of self-doubt. However, the Northern deserter slinks through the mist and moss and gloom and discovers her. 'All alone, little lady?' He attempts to grab her; she throws him off, snatches the gun hidden in the back of the wagon and hides it behind her. The villain comes towards her with evil intent. At the last minute she whips out the gun and shoots him in the right eyeball. He whirls around and in a split second applies a blood sponge to his eye. As he hits the front, the spotlight glitters on the blood pouring from his shattered face and he drops down dead (preferably not in the horseshit).

Scarlett calms Melanie and the baby, bravely declares with barely a tremor, 'We're going home, to Tara' and leads the horse and wagon offstage as the music swells. Not a dry eye in the house.

It was fun playing evil and I could even cope with the bloody horse, but what do you do when you head toward your victim and her gun jams? During the run at Drury Lane, it happened perhaps twice in eighteen months; over in America it seemed to happen nearly every other performance. I don't know where this myth about American technological wizardry came from. I lost faith in it forever when Jimmy Carter's helicopters crashed into each other in the desert, but surely the one thing they'd know about would be guns, for heaven's sake? Not so. I kept having to have unexplained heart attacks. One time, when the crew had decided that Leslie Ann needed a hair trigger to solve her inability to shoot the thing, she grabbed it from the wagon, hid it behind her and promptly shot herself in the bustle. She shrieked, dropped the gun, and frantically slapped her behind to put out the sparks. I, meanwhile, sighed and had yet another heart attack. Judging from the hysteria coming across the footlights from the audience, the spectators were deeply moved.

Chapter 13

Glamour in the Hollywood hills…drugs and brownies…Scrooge and the Mafia…sight-reading with Robert Merrill…home on a wing and a prayer

ALTHOUGH THE Los Angeles season had been a trifle hairy professionally, it had been terrific outside performance hours. The weather stayed perfect the entire time. This was mid-winter but I was able to keep topping up my tan beside the pool. The company was 'at home' and anxious to keep me amused and entertained. The Americans, particularly on the West Coast it seems, are remarkably generous and hospitable. Of course, it helps if you are in work and have any influence, however small, in their ever-pressing search for jobs. When word got round Hollywood that I was looking for extras to lie about as victims in the aftermath of the razing of Atlanta, I was the toast of every bar in town!

Unforgettably, I lived out the fantasy of 'the party in the Hollywood hills.' A well-known choreographer had a pre-Christmas bash miles up above the town in his extraordinary glass-fronted edifice. The enormous galleried front reception room went up two stories where a silver and blue decorated Christmas tree, roughly the size of the one in Trafalgar Square, reaching the ceiling. Lights twinkled below as far as the eye could see and famous faces twinkled near at hand with as much animation as their facelifts would allow. At one point the host asked if anyone fancied watching a movie and an entire wall rose up to become a cinema-sized screen. Three or four people then settled down to enjoy *Singin' in the Rain*.

I, meanwhile, was engaging in small talk with the rich and famous and trying to look as if I belonged in this world. Refreshments were set out tastefully and I was beside a table with a very tempting tray of chocolate brownies. As I chatted I would reach behind me for a nibble or so of the delicious confections. Gradually, however, I realised that although I could see the mouths moving of the people around me, I had become stone deaf. Then I found myself stuck in one position and unable to make my muscles work. I felt like a Victorian exhibit in a glass bell. How was I, an innocent abroad, to know that the plate of brownies contained a whole 'head' of marihuana? I was told later that I was picked up, still stuck in my frozen position like a dead budgie, and laid to rest in a spare bedroom. I woke up four hours later totally refreshed and unharmed, but afflicted with a terminal case of un-coolness.

That, my friends, is my total involvement in the drug scene through a long and otherwise eventful life. I suppose I'll remain uncool to the end.

On we went to San Francisco. The problem was that the Curran is a much smaller theatre than the Dorothy Chandler and none of the sets fitted. The happy American crew did three straight days and nights at 'Golden Time' (triple pay!!) to cut and mix and match to squeeze them in. They finally managed and we had a nice time in the super city but the tour was doomed. Two reasons, really. The first was the obvious problem with the set, which would have to be modified drastically to get in most of the booked venues, and secondly, Fielding's failure to convince American Equity to agree to June Ritchie replacing Ms Warren. He was certain that June's performance would catapult the show into the major hit status. Despite all the pleas and threats, however, Equity stayed firm.

This is always a difficult area and both sides of the Atlantic have been guilty of overprotectiveness in the past. In this case, however, by saving Ms Warren's blushes, Harold made good his threat to pull out of the tour and about eighty American Equity members lost their jobs.

As had I. What to do to make a bit of spare dosh to take home? I know, I'll help the Mafia launder some hot money. I jest, I jest!! These were all just wicked and baseless allegations made during and after the event. I'm absolutely sure that those charming Italian gentlemen spending thousands and thousands of dollars producing a show to run for three weeks in a 30,000-seat arena and then forgetting to publicise it, did so from the purest of motives.

The show was called *Scrooge*, not the relatively tasteful film version I was in a decade later with Albert Finney, Kenneth More, Alec Guinness,

Edith Evans et al, but a remarkably twee and putrid version written by an American housewife. The venue was the elegantly named San Francisco Cow Palace where the huge political Conventions are apt to be celebrated in election years. To waste (pardon me) invest as much money as possible, five complete stages were built on the floor of the arena, each complete with lighting and sound. No sets had to change, the actors moved from one to another, which would then light up, on cue. The whole centre of the vast space was a London park complete with working fountain.

The cast was led by John Carradine, famous since starring in the original *Stagecoach* with John Wayne and father of the Carradine boys that crop up on television now and then. Playing his nephew for some unfathomable reason (well, $8000 a performance, eight times a week possibly made a difference) was Robert Merrill, the then leading baritone of the Metropolitan Opera. Curiously, the show also had a Nativity scene at the end of the first act with every wild animal you could think of paraded through the London park.

The dancers, as is usual, started rehearsing a week before the rest of the cast. We were working on the 'Gold Ballet' where we flitted about in skintight gold lamé bodytights representing Scrooge's unhealthy interest in money. I kid you not! The following Monday Mr Carradine was supposed to have driven himself up from Hollywood for rehearsals but, with his arthritis and all, had to stop over halfway. The trouble was that Mr Merrill, whose time was precious, was there waiting to rehearse with him.

Who was Mr Carradine's understudy? You guessed it. Old habits die hard. Mid-morning Monday the stage manager came running down the corridor, grabbed me and dragged me along to the other rehearsal hall. We were rehearsing underneath the arena in huge aircraft hangars with those enormous sliding steel doors. We stopped outside to catch our breath and then slid back the great door. There, in the middle distance, was a grand piano. Standing beside it baton in hand was the distinguished conductor hired for the occasion. Beyond it ranged in rows on chairs in an arc was a chorus of some eighty singers that I hadn't yet met. Finally, lounging negligently against the piano was the leading baritone of the Metropolitan Opera. The stage manager looked at me, pointed dramatically to the waiting company and said, 'GO IN THERE AND SIGHT READ THE DUET WITH MR MERRILL.'

I still remember the sound of my shoes as I went clip, clop, clip over to the distant group. I still remember my heart beating unnaturally in my throat. I still remember the cold sweat. I felt like Jimmy Cagney heading for the electric chair in a gangster movie. However, I survived, as one does, and Mr Merrill (call me Bob!) was charming. 'If only dear Johnnie could sing it as well as that when he comes.' Yeah, sure!

We opened to some thirty odd people scattered about the echoing arena. We ran for two of the scheduled three weeks and were paid off for the third. Strangely, the meeting when it was announced that the show was coming off had a totally different feel than on similar occasions. Although the producers paid suitable lip-service to the sadness they felt at losing all of us, the sound of satisfied hands rubbing together seemed not all that far away.

Right, I'd made my little pile of extra dough, now to get home. This wasn't as easy as it would appear. Mr Fielding had flown me over one-way as the final date on the tour couldn't be certain. When he heard that I'd stayed on to do another show, he invoked the Equity rule stating that the artist must catch the designated 'company plane' after an engagement or the producer is off the hook. I admired his gall if nothing else. There was no company, only little me. What possible difference did it make which particular plane one person flew on? Legally, of course, he held all the cards and my threat to turn up in his office dripping wet and hung about with seaweed had little effect.

So I found a bucket shop. This offered a one-way LA-to-London ticket at a real knockdown price. Super! It seemed a bit strange when the office had disappeared the next day, but I was told on the telephone to make my way down the coast to Hollywood, which was fine as my friends in the company were going home and I could bum a lift. Then I had to rendezvous at a house in North Hollywood at ten in the evening. I was more than a trifle nervous by this time but I arrived at the designated address and rang the bell. The door opened to reveal a large Indian party in full swing. India-type Indian, not Native American. I asked for my contact who shortly arrived at the door a trifle worse for wear, but clutching my ticket in his hand. Vastly relieved as I was leaving the following morning, I didn't examine it carefully until I was on my way to the airport. I then discovered that this was the return half of a ticket and the name of a Mr Singh could be deciphered under mine. Oh, God! I spent the entire trip in a blind panic but not an eyebrow was raised at either end. I arrived home vowing never again to deviate from the straight and narrow, but, when all is said and done, a bargain is a bargain!

Chapter 14

*Films and more films…bundles to Britain…Jeanne Moreau and Peter O'Toole…dancing in the rain…*Chitty Chitty *and Dick Van Dyke*

I HATE LISTS. I thought I should write about the films I was involved in, but it's far too much like work to try to remember which came when, so I'll concentrate on the bits I remember as they come to mind and not worry too much about chronological order. There were just over a dozen in all, squeezed in and around the West End shows. Some of them were even pretty good! Most of them, however…

The whole point about dancing in pictures was that you have absolutely no responsibility for their ultimate success or failure. Naturally, you work hard and perform to the best of your ability, but once finished, you collect your money and run. A stage show is an ongoing commitment and the punters mightn't come back again the next night. A movie is forgotten once the last shot is in the can. It's obviously important to the stars, directors and producers whether the thing bombs or not, but to us, the length of the contract and the cheque at the end of the week are the only real considerations. Whether the flick is good, bad or indifferent has nothing whatever to do with the enjoyment factor in making it. Some of my best times were had on turkeys.

The nice thing about the early films was the time it took to do anything. The cameras were huge cumbersome monsters and tracks had to be laid for each shot so they could roll along smoothly. This meant a lot of sitting around, a lot of gossip, a good deal of flirting and some high-powered on-going poker games.

(That reminds me, I'm a frighteningly lucky poker player. During the twelve weeks we ran *Gone with the Wind* in the States a group of actors, mainly the black cast with a few of us whites, had a running poker game every night between scenes. During the entire run I

NEVER LOST! I became known as 'Bundles to Britain.' They were very good about it and when word spread round the company of my exploits, they put together a plan to send me to Lake Tahoe to gamble for them! They were seriously going to pool their resources and set me loose in the casino. Being convinced I was sure to lose all their money, I assured them that I wasn't the Continental card sharp they thought I was and bowed out. I'm actually quite frightened of gambling. I think I could become overly fond of the activity very quickly.)

Back to the pictures. The profligate idiocy involved in the business was evident from the very beginning. In *Follow a Star* Eleanor Fazan taught me Norman Wisdom's number as his 'dance in' to show the cameramen what was involved. The designer was very proud of a lovingly polished, huge, mahogany boardroom table acquired from Heals, the very grand department store, for £400 as a centrepiece of the set. This was an enormous sum in the 1950s. At the climax of the number, the star jumps up and cavorts madly about on the gleaming tabletop. Come the camera rehearsal, despite my reservations, I did the number as choreographed and, naturally, totally ruined the expensive table. The designer, in tears, heads back to Heals. You learn very quickly, however, never to say, 'I told you so.'

There were some magical moments through the years. I did a curious little film for Paddy Stone called *Great Catherine*, with Jeanne Moreau and Peter O'Toole, about Catherine of Russia. We were a band of Cossacks who raided her palace and roughed up the aristocrats. Butch? You betcha! Mme Moreau liked to sit around and gossip between takes rather than retire to her trailer. She would sit and knit in the Continental manner with one needle immobile under her left arm. Although she was dressed in full court dress and tiara, she looked like a nice, homely, French peasant woman sitting on her doorstep. I happened to be watching her when the assistant director came to tell her she was wanted on set. She then put down her knitting, stood up and literally became beautiful. It was quite extraordinary. As she prepared herself internally for the take, you'd swear that her very bone structure changed.

Mr O'Toole was quite another matter. He was part of the musical number, which involved us throwing him about violently. Paddy choreographed it carefully and I stood in for O'Toole to rehearse it so that it was as safe as possible. The problem was that he was so spaced out at that point in his career that he came out of his dressing-room smiling dreamily and resolutely refused to rehearse. All those hours of practice went for nought; he just became a rag doll and cheerfully let us do with him as we would. It worked perfectly well; maybe substance abuse has its uses after all.

I've previously touched on *Half a Sixpence*. Although it eventually got too big for its boots, in my opinion, it was professionally made and the numbers were fun to do. The only real problem came in making 'If the rain's got to fall.' Rain just doesn't show on screen unless it's pelting down with great force. The number was shot at Henley in a clearing in the trees beside the Thames. To create enough rain to make an impression, we were ringed about with firemen on ladders using their most powerful hoses with water pumped straight from the river. We would get into position for the shot, the director would yell, 'Cue the rain' and we would immediately be soaked to the skin in freezing water. Then, and only then, would the lighting cameraman make final adjustments and decide whether he should wait for a particular fluffy cloud to come into view before the playback could be cued to start the shot. While we waited, shivering with ague and plotting to kill whoever had this bright idea in the first place, we were urged by Gillian Lynne to remember to keep smiling and above all to keep our eyes open. Have you ever tried to keep smiling and your eyes open while being knocked off your feet by a fireman's hose?

We started shooting the song in mid-September and the late summer scenery looked lovely. As the gallons of water soaked in, however, the beautiful green sward became a bog and was replaced with green painted concrete. Then the leaves started to turn colour and were sprayed a fresh green every morning. It's quite fun watching the scene now and trying to separate the real from the cosmetic.

Chitty Chitty was very odd because although the two numbers we had in the film, the 'Toot Sweet' factory number and 'Me Old Bamboo', appear in the first quarter of an hour in the picture, they were done at either end of the shoot. We started by rehearsing very hard for a fortnight for the Hollywood choreographers and were having a well-earned break one day, sitting flaked out around the edges of the room. Suddenly the double doors at the far end burst open and a manic figure came tumbling down the length of the hall, cartwheels, flips, somersaults, ending in a knee slide to the choreographers' table. Taa-raa!! This was Mr Van Dyke making his entrance. I'm afraid the world-weary British dancers sitting about glanced up, perhaps raised an eyebrow or two, and went back to their newspapers.

Once we got onto the wonderful Ken Adam set, we had great fun learning to spin those black iron trolley things and started to shoot the number. I negotiated a £5 chit as James Robertson Justice's dance-in every time we rehearsed the last bit when he walks through the scene, so everything was tickety-boo. We got to the end in good order and filmed the chaos with the vats of goo spilling and all the dogs rushing in. We thought we'd finished the number. To our surprise we were called in the next day for more of the same. In the film there's only about half a minute of all this happening but we kept doing this stuff for days. It turned out that Dick Van Dyke had twisted his ankle and couldn't work but 'sshh, the insurance types mustn't find this out or they might close down the picture,' so we kept shooting more and more unnecessary bits and pieces while he recovered. There must be enough footage lying around somewhere of us sliding around in the muck, being snapped at by the ever more irritated pack of dogs, to make a slapstick documentary.

Thankfully, as I've mentioned, we went home and sat around all summer waiting to be called for the other number. Some of the dancers really cashed in by moonlighting on *Oliver!* as well. The contracts ran out in the autumn and had to be renewed, as they still hadn't got to the fairground number. When they did, we filmed it quite quickly and that should have been that. The visa of the American assistant to the choreographers ran out, however, and they asked me to extend my contract yet again to replace him. I finally finished behind the camera for the old professor's number. I spent the best part of a year on the epic and it was interesting and lucrative, and, of course, it went on to be a huge hit, but for sheer inspired lunacy nothing could compare with the year spent on what is officially considered one of the twenty worst movies of all time, *Song of Norway.*

Chapter 15

*Song of Norway…freezing on a train…rehearsals in London,
shooting in Scandinavia…stuck above the clouds…Yakima Knutt
and the runaway hay wagon…overtime in kroner*

ANDREW AND VIRGINIA STONE were veteran Hollywood producer/
directors who had the 'bright' idea of turning the creaky 1944
Broadway musical about the life of Edvard Grieg into a blockbusting
Todd-AO spectacle. The Norwegians were appalled; the composer is a
revered national hero and they feared it would turn out to be vulgar and
tacky. Surely not!!! They were slightly mollified by the casting of Toralv
Maurstad, one of their leading actors, in the title role. His only problem
was that he was a good twenty years too old for the early scenes (and
no, the blonde wig didn't help).

The Stones brought with them from America Florence Henderson, a
sort of sit-com version of Julie Andrews, to play his wife, and a young
actor/singer called Frank Poretta to play Grieg's oldest friend. He was
the proper age for the beginning stuff, but, as Toralv grew into the right
age, Frank grew out of it. They made a curious pair of life-long buddies.
They also brought along a couple of American male dancers, in case we
turned out to be lousy, and the choreographer, a feisty little lady called
Lee Theodore.

The rest of the cast featured the continental actors, Christina
Schollin and Oscar Homolka, the very British Robert Morley, Elizabeth
Larner and Harry Secombe and, of all people, Edward G. Robinson! All
the actors involved spoke English, of a sort, but no attempt was made
to match accent with role. Much of the guilty fun in watching the
thing is to hear a supposedly close-knit group of Norwegians talking
animatedly, more or less, in three or four different versions of the same
language. My favourite is the mid-western American twang that sits so
elegantly in the nineteenth century Norwegian musical setting.

While the second unit was sent over to Norway to shoot stunning aerial shots of the beautiful country, (one of the few real successes of the film, it's a glorious travelogue) the dancing crew, plus the American additions, started rehearsing in London. It's rather difficult simulating a mountaintop or a boat on a fjord in Covent Garden, but we learned the steps and heard about the 250 Norwegian folk dancers of all ages that were to join us in the big scenes. After being sent out to buy thermal underwear and heavy-duty winter gear, we flew out to shoot the winter wonderland sequences. Filmed in the Lillehammer area which would later host the winter Olympics, there was very little dancing involved in all this; it mostly involved jolly troika rides, snowball fights and frolicking in the snow with our new Norwegian friends (the aforementioned folk dancers.) They were all in their traditional costumes and we couldn't understand how the girls in particular withstood the extreme temperature in their flimsy blouses.

It all became clear later when we sat in compartments with them on an antique train trundling back and forth shooting Mr Secombe's arrival at a country station. The train was from an outdoor railway museum. It dated from about 1890 and the compartments we were sitting in hadn't been opened for half a century. It brought a new meaning to the words freezing cold. I was brought up in Canada, for heaven's sake, it should all have been a piece of cake, but there was something about the icy tomblike atmosphere that chilled the blood. We couldn't stop our teeth from chattering, but the Norwegians in their blouses and dirndl skirts were perfectly at ease and having a wonderful time. They finally took pity on us and offered us their secret weapon. Aquavit! Concealed somewhere about the person of every Norwegian extra was a supply of the delicious homemade liqueur of the country. Those wily Norwegians were getting through the day in this outdoor refrigerator warmed and comforted by being ever-so-slightly sloshed.

We had several weeks of this, being royally entertained by our new friends in the evenings and even learning how to do their traditional dances. It was a million miles away from the big smoke of London, but eventually we found ourselves back home to rehearse for the spring and summer sequences.

These were more intensive, as this time we would actually have to dance, rather than just hurl snowballs and mime to a playback, while waving gamely from a freezing train. After a few weeks of enjoyable work we flew back to Scandinavia. Rehearsals are often the most intensively satisfying work on a job of this nature. Once you hit the location the dancing tends to be dissipated as you make allowances for slippery grass or stony ground, but as long as the choreographer knows his/her stuff, the creative process can be stimulating. Although I've worked with a few unmentionables in my time, where you spend your entire time making their pretentious crap look passable, I've been mainly very lucky with the people I've danced for. Lee was fine. She had played Anybody's in the Broadway *West Side* and was firm but fair.

We spent a lot of time shooting in Aarhus, Denmark, in the village museum. It was a clever idea. The Danes had scoured the country for antique buildings in danger of collapse and had brought them all together and rebuilt them brick by brick to form a sort of living folk museum. Not only is it a lively tourist attraction but also it was perfect for shooting a period film. No more worrying about television aerials or other modern accoutrements.

It was after finishing in Aarhus and starting to fly around Norway from location to location that the fun really started. The main problem with any large-scale production is, of course, the weather. If you start shooting a large musical number in bright sunshine, say, you have to have the same sort of weather for the length of time it takes to finish it. Naturally, every schedule overruns. The problem escalates if the next location is picked for a particular feature that is only evident for a limited time. One beautiful valley had a stunning vista of apple blossom up one whole side of a mountain. We arrived just as the flowers were starting to fall. Twelve dozen gross of plastic apple blossom were sent over from London to bolster the rapidly disappearing effect.

Our favourite time came when we began to shoot a number on a boat in a fjord. The stars and crew were billeted down in the village on the waterside. We were put into an out of season ski lodge high up on the mountain overlooking the fjord. We were perfectly happy, especially when the weather closed in making shooting impossible. The point is, the clouds settled down *below* us. The poor big shots were waking up every morning to dark, overcast, miserable days while we had glorious sunshine above the clouds. It was like being on an aeroplane. This carried on for some time. Nothing could be done until the clouds lifted so we lazed around, ate the rather bland but nourishing Norwegian cuisine, and went for long walks in the beautiful countryside.

On one of these strolls, a group of us came upon a particularly inviting pool. It was perfectly circular and crystal clear. We'd been walking for some time and had worked up a sweat, the weather was hot and still, so we decided to have a dip. As we were all alone up on our mountain, we had no hesitation in stripping off. The ever-eager Michelle Hardy, a lively dancer and old friend who still brings her wonderful energy and enthusiasm to her work as a choreographer, shouted, 'I'll go first, I'll go first!' She then took a long run at the pool and plunged in. There was a tiny pause and then Michelle came straight up out of the water looking like an irate water nymph in her scanties and screaming blue murder. The pool turned out to be an only just melted bit of glacier. After we managed to stop laughing, we got Ms Hardy out and dried her off.

When the weather lifted, we started on the boat number. We would be picked up early in the morning and driven down to the pier by bus. We would embark and have make-up and hair done while chugging to the prettiest location on the fjord. We would get a few hours' shooting in until the sun moved behind the mountain and the whole exercise went into reverse. As our official day started the minute we left our hotel and overtime would kick in on our way back up, someone would look at his watch on the way, do a few calculations and yell, 'Once more round the mountain, George!'

Filming the runaway hay wagon was fairly traumatic. A group of us were being driven down a mountain in a wagon drawn by four horses which then break away and we plunge out of control downhill. The legendary stunt man, Yakima Knutt, however, was managing the wagon. This great man had invented and performed the stunt supposedly done by John Wayne in *Stagecoach* where he dropped under the speeding coach and worked his way underneath to the other end and re-emerged to confound the bad guys. Harrison Ford revived it years later for *Indiana Jones*. In our case he lay on a specially built platform under the hay wagon and steered it down the mountain on his stomach. We all had doubles and were only supposed to do a short run for close-ups. When the time came, however, they just let it rip. I suppose it would be too difficult to stop it halfway. The shrieks and screams were all too genuine. They couldn't use much of it, however, as our false moustaches and sideburns were blown off by the tearing wind.

When we finally finished the great work we were paid all our overtime in local kroner. I brought mine home in a brown paper bag. I handed it over to my kindly bank manager who converted it for me bit by bit. It was enough for me to install central heating in the Ightham house! I've changed my mind. Forget the accents and the melodrama; I hereby nominate *Song of Norway* as the greatest film of all time.

Chapter 16

*Hoofing for Gillie…*Hans Andersen *at the Palladium…big news
in the Turkish bath…co-starring with Tommy Steele…partner to
Dame Anna Neagle and looking after* My Fair Lady

BACK FROM THE tinsel and glitter of California safe and sound
with the dodgy airline ticket safely disposed of, I looked around
for the next job. We've now reached the mid 1970s and I've reached
my late thirties and was just beginning to wonder how long I
could compete on equal terms with the younger dancers coming up.
When I heard that Gillian Lynne was choreographing *Hans Andersen*
with Tommy Steele for a run at the Palladium I decided to test the
waters.

I didn't ring Gillie about it; I just turned up at the audition, dance
bag over my shoulder, got changed and hoofed my way through the day
alongside kids of half my age. Gillie looked a bit quizzical, but went
along with it; not a word was spoken. She set a lot of tough
combinations and I satisfied myself that I could still cut it. That being
settled, I agreed to be her assistant and to understudy the Irish actor
Milo O'Shea. Milo played Otto, the second lead in the show opposite
Tommy. Otto was Andersen's guide and mentor throughout and it's
never made quite explicit whether the character is real or somehow
magical. Milo was certainly magical in the part but during the year we
ran at the Palladium was never off.

As the run neared its close, negotiations were taking place for the
National Tour. Tommy and all the other distinguished principal
supporting actors in the show, Colette Gleason, Lila Kaye, Bob Todd,
Geoffrey Toone etc. agreed to go. The one exception was Milo, who
wanted his wife to replace Colette as Jenny Lind. The producers,
Fielding again, refused, so he was leaving at the end of the London run.
This was of little concern to me, as Fielding would insist on a name in
such a leading role. Tommy was to redirect it himself and had casting

As Otto in Hans Andersen.

approval. He had spent the last month interviewing various leading players but couldn't make up his mind.

We were now in the last week of the run and things were getting a bit tight, although not panicking, as there was a three-week rehearsal period before embarking on the tour. I was getting a head start by rehearsing the replacement dancers and had called a Tuesday morning rehearsal. I put them through their paces and decided to get a bit of steam in the afternoon to iron out the kinks before the evening performance. Accordingly, I was sitting relaxing in a Turkish bath at about teatime when the door opened and David Freeman, the stage manager, in full suit and tie, peered through the billowing steam and naked bodies. 'Paddy, are you in there? Sorry to bother you but Milo's got food poisoning. You're on tonight.'

'Ooooh' went the unclad assembled company. 'Good luck…Break a leg…Give 'em hell.'

I accompanied the sweating David back to the Palladium and made some quick decisions. No, I didn't want him to call Tommy in. As in the *West Side* incident, if there isn't time to rehearse properly, don't start, you'll only panic (or your co-star will). Besides, I felt I knew Tommy by this time. He's an excellent instinctive actor and likes a bit of danger. I also knew my strengths and weaknesses. For one thing there was no possibility of me playing the role in Milo's style. He was a short Irish actor of great charm and experience. I was a tall mid-Atlantic dancer/actor with a rather quirky style and a bit of chutzpah.

I decided to go out with all guns blazing and have some fun. What could they do, sack me? It was the last week of the run. Every scene the character plays is opposite Mr Steele, so from the beginning I hit on the magical and theatrical qualities inherent in the part, hopefully staying just this side of over the top, and threw in the odd ad-lib or two to keep Tommy guessing. I had a ball!

Now the fat was in the fire. Tommy insisted I play it on tour. Harold Fielding objected violently. He had two concerns: 1. I didn't have a name to help pull in the punters. 2. You can't have the second lead billed under the other well-known character actors. Harold raged, Tommy was adamant. Harold pleaded, Tommy stonewalled. I just sat on the sidelines and giggled. As the whole thing was totally unexpected, I felt I had nothing to lose and just waited to hear the final bell. Tommy pulled the old 'If he doesn't go, neither do I' routine, and although no one believed him for a minute, Harold wearily caved in. I happily accepted lowest billing on the principals' totem pole and we were on our way.

I suddenly realized that after all those years of playing for other people, I was about to embark on a major National tour in a mammoth musical playing opposite one of Britain's best loved stars AS ME!! Was I intimidated? Was I struck with stage fright? Was I properly humble and grateful for the chance? NO WAY!! I felt like Ethel Merman in the finale of *Gypsy*. Those roses were finally coming up (and about bloody time!)

Tommy was remarkably generous in the rehearsal period before we left on tour. He restaged several of the scenes between us and always to my benefit. There's a song Otto sings to Hans early in the piece when they've been thrown in prison, for instance. At this distance I can't for the life of me remember what it was about. Presumably something uplifting about keeping one's spirits up or whatever. In the original version, Milo sat on a bale of hay and sang it to Hans sitting downstage left. Tommy changed it so that he sat downstage centre with his back to the audience so I could sing it straight out front. Mind you, after we'd been touring for a few months and had settled comfortably into the roles, he'd use the opportunity to pull faces in an attempt to make me corpse, but that was all to come.

We opened in Manchester. I shared a principal's dressing-room with the very dignified Geoffrey Toone. He must have been in his sixties at this point and tended to play aristocratic judges, but in the early 1950s had been a huge hit in the West End wearing next to nothing in the comedy *The Little Hut*. This exposure, to coin a phrase, had taken him over to Hollywood, so we could spend hours comparing notes on the place. I must say his celebrities could always trump mine.

I got my first review! The Manchester critic called me 'a constant pleasure.' Wow! I didn't even mind when this prompted Geoffrey and the others to nickname me Constance for a time. However, this was the one and only time when I was almost persuaded to abandon my hardheaded Rules. Remember rule 6 in Chapter 12? If not, see me in detention later. I did have a photographer come up to Manchester and do a photo shoot. I did send résumés round to various acting agencies. I did get a bit above myself. There were six months to go on the tour, however, so nothing could happen in a hurry. I just settled down to enjoy myself.

Tommy as star and director did not go down too well with all the cast members. Affectionately known as 'that little shit' by some, his habit of firing off notes in all directions after a performance did not win many friends. He was that most maddening of creatures, a perfectionist in his demands on others, but capable of the most evil behaviour himself. He would claim to be under the weather and not at all certain whether he would make the performance. His understudy would be costumed and made-up and waiting nervously in the wings when our star would brush by at the last minute having dressed in his hotel room. Funny? Well…

*Head of the table at a Toronto luncheon with Richard Caldicott (Colonel Pickering)
and Dame Anna Neagle (Mrs Higgins) during the tour of* My Fair Lady.

To me, however, he was sweetness and light. I was his blue-eyed boy,
his discovery, and could walk on water. Our last scene together in the
show was well-constructed and effective. Otto has guided Hans from
being a village cobbler through many vicissitudes to being accepted as a
world famous writer and the time has come for him to stand on his
own. I deliver my final speech, walk to upstage right, turn for a final
farewell, and disappear. Hans waits for my exit round, turns front and
sings his last inspired song through glistening eyes and the final curtain
falls. One night well into the run, this scene caused Tommy to write my
one and only note during the entire tour. 'I don't mind at all your
having a nice round of applause on your final exit, but I do object to
cheers!!'

Oh, it was tempting. It would have been so easy to lay claim to being
an actor now and hold out for roles that 'suited my status.' When the
tour came to an end, Peg was perfectly willing to find nourishing
recipes for dandelion soup and back me all the way, but then Gillie
called with a wild idea.

There was a very young enthusiastic producer called Cameron

Mackintosh who had managed to persuade the Arts Council to join him in a scheme to try to keep the big provincial theatres in business. They had been complaining for years that the big stars were refusing to tour any more and they couldn't draw in the customers. Cameron's ploy, funded by the Arts Council, was to produce a lavish production of *My Fair Lady*, mount it in Leicester and send it round the country. Where did I come in? Well, he had persuaded Dame Anna Neagle to play Mrs Higgins and the idea was to give her a special dancing spot in the ballroom scene. If I agreed to partner her, I could do my bit every night with the lovely Dame Anna and then look after the show on the road. By giving up my impractical notions of becoming the new Olivier and agreeing to this little proposition, I set in train a series of events that would shape the rest of my career.

Chapter 17

Peg as Warden of the hill…learning Ancient Greek…first signs of Parkinson's…working with Alan J. Lerner…ditto James Hammerstein…the best opening night present ever

ALL THOSE TIMES while I was gallivanting hither and thither on tours or on film locations, Peg had been holding the family together down in Kent. She became Warden of the woods behind the house for the National Trust. Her duties were not onerous, mainly involving a walk up her beloved hill once a day accompanied by Darcy, our huge but soppy Alsatian. She would report anything amiss, such as abandoned cars or the like, and her token emolument took care of his dog food. She loved her garden and would potter away for hours. I would do the grand gestures such as planting a yew hedge that I was assured would take years to mature. The idiot thing shot up at a rate of knots and I very shortly found myself up high ladders practising topiary.

She continued to write, but despite immediately acquiring a highly respected and enthusiastic London literary agent, never sold over here in England. It must have been immensely frustrating for her. She would do a script for television, for instance, and the BBC would rave about its freshness and feign intense interest in it. They would then sit on it for months, have a whole series of meetings about it and then, regretfully, decide not to do it after all. How she kept her insouciance is a mystery. She was a voracious reader and had lots of little ploys and devices to allow her to continue to read while she bathed, did the washing up, the housework or watched television. At one point she decided that she needed to read the Odyssey and the Iliad in the original Greek. David, the language scholar, assured her that it would be impossible to teach yourself Ancient Greek without the benefit of a Romance language first. Peg, like me, had little or no formal education, but proved David wrong. Years later she created a sensation in a taverna in a Greek village by reciting a stanza from Homer to the astonished locals.

Just before I was to leave for *Fair Lady* Peg noticed that her long-standing slight tremor was getting more tiresome. She had always had a problem with teacups and the like on stage, but nothing particular to worry about. Now, however, she was getting aches in her right shoulder as well. I took her to our local GP, (the one-time lead in *Devil's Disciple*) who recommended a London specialist. Nothing appeared to be urgent or dramatic so I went up to Leicester to rehearse. A few weeks later, after the show had opened, Peg called to say that the specialist had the results of her tests and that she had Parkinson's disease.

Neither of us had the slightest idea what this meant and the doctors made great play of this only being one-sided Parkinson's. She was young to have had it diagnosed and the progression was to be very gradual. She had the ghastly thing for twelve years, but it was only the last eighteen months or so that were truly horrific. For the time being, apart from some fairly minor irritations, life carried on as usual. (Notice I said 'as usual.' Am I the only person in the world who deplores the almost universal use of 'as normal?' To my mind you can say that something carries on as usual or carries on normally, but you can't say as normal! God, I'm getting old and pedantic.)

Up in Leicester the show opened in triumph and did, indeed, pull in the audiences on the tour. Robin Midgley directed it and he and I collaborated on a Victorian Christmas show in the Studio Theatre in Leicester while *Fair Lady* ran in the main house. I put together a proper Harlequinade as one of my first choreographic efforts. Back in London, however, the great Alan J. Lerner decided he'd like to re-direct *Fair Lady* himself for the West End and I became his Associate Director as well as still assisting Gillie.

When, predictably I suppose, Alan fell in love with his charming leading lady, Liz Robertson, who later became the eighth Mrs Lerner, I found myself rehearsing all the big scenes while Alan concentrated on his new Eliza. I danced with Dame Anna on the opening night and then handed over to my understudy while I concentrated on keeping the show fresh and taking rehearsal calls. What with the cast changes and the first, second and even third understudies needed for some of the roles, I directed thirteen Elizas during its four-year run.

Never wanting to do anything by halves, Cameron decided to repeat the whole exercise with *Oklahoma!*. This was to be directed by James

Hammerstein, son of Oscar, and I was to be his Associate Director. Gemse de Lappe came over from America to reproduce Agnes de Mille's original choreography. Back we went to Leicester but this was not to be the easy, seamless exercise that the first show had been.

Cameron recently mounted a splendid *Oklahoma!* for the National Theatre that went on to a successful run at the Lyceum, but back in 1980 when our version came in to the Palace Theatre, he wasn't allowed the artistic freedom that made this latest version such a success. Back then the Hammersteins had total control of professional productions of the Rodgers and Hammerstein musicals. One of the provisos was that the original choreography was used. Cameron thought that some of it – particularly 'Kansas City,' the tap number – had dated. Once we were on tour, he would bring in Gillian Lynne to pep things up. She would re-rehearse numbers, Jamie would come back to see it, hate it, and change it all back again. I was in the middle, trying to keep everyone happy.

When we finally opened at the Palace, it was after a very trying and troublesome tour. There had been a lot of problems with casting. The Ado Annie character was replaced in mid-tour and it was agreed that some chorus members would need changing before the West End opening. At the end of the tour, Cameron sent me up to Bristol, the last date. I was made to sit in the company office between shows on the last Saturday and have the cast in one at a time to tell them whether they were going to the West End. 'Yes, you're coming.' 'No, you're not.' I came out to a cartoon on the notice board of me standing over a gory pile of bodies dripping blood.

We arrived back in London and re-cast, including the leading lady who was allegedly fired by Richard Rodgers' widow because she couldn't reliably hit the top B flat in 'People Will Say We're In Love.' That was the only thing missing from her entire, enchanting performance. It had been cleverly re-orchestrated but Mrs Rodgers apparently asserted that no one could open in London without that top B flat and that was that.

However, we finally struggled to the opening night at the Palace. Jamie Hammerstein and I were standing on stage before the half-hour was called. It was all very quiet and calm for a change. Jamie was a charming and polite east-coast American, very tall, very academic looking with glasses and a rather shy manner. He looked at me, shuffled his feet a bit, and said 'Paddy, I'd like to give you an opening-night present.' I replied, 'Oh, that's kind of you, Jamie', and expected him to produce a bottle of champagne perhaps, or, being a Hammerstein, maybe a crate, you never know! However, he shuffled a bit more and said, 'I'd like to give you 1.5 per cent of the gross.' Now I don't know how much this would mean to non-theatre people, but I was totally and absolutely staggered. 1.5 per cent of the gross of the box office take of the Palace Theatre in London represented a great deal of money to someone in my position. Cameron Mackintosh was more than a little miffed when he found out about it, because he was already paying me two salaries, one for looking after *Oklahoma* and one for looking after *My Fair Lady* at the Adelphi. Also it's very, very 'not done' for non-essential people to see the actual gross of the theatre take, which might or might not agree with the published publicity. I would receive the show report every week from Jamie's agent, however, with my percentage cheque enclosed. It was the nicest theatrical gesture I've ever heard of and I'll always be grateful to Jamie. I just wish that show had run forever!

Chapter 18

Looking after two West End shows…trying to change career direction…getting my Bachelor of Arts…Cameron Mackintosh modernizes his office…House Manager of the refurbished Old Vic…first Queen Mother occasion

ONCE THE TWO SHOWS were running in London and I'd sorted out a rehearsal schedule for the respective understudies, as well as a fairly loose plan of action to keep an eye on key moments in the performances based on the length of time it takes to walk between the two theatres, life settled into a routine. I'd been thinking for some time that I would soon need to move into something that didn't require either constant touring or throwing the legs about, so it was decision time, particularly as the progression of Peg's illness was unpredictable. Goodness knows I'd had plenty of false starts.

When the painful realization that I couldn't go on being a lithe and lissom young dancer forever first hit me, a few years previously, I could still, as it were, do it. I had no shortage of jobs. I had also done a fair bit of choreographing and directing (of which more later) but I had no faith that I could count on the continuous employment I needed. I obviously wanted to stay connected to the theatre, so I decided to start with back-stage management. I thought that this was probably the simplest way to crossover and to do that I would need basic experience. Accordingly, I answered an advertisement in *The Stage* placed by the Canterbury Theatre. They were looking for a backstage assistant-cum-stage manager with various other duties and it seemed just the right sort of thing for me to start with. I had made my decision and was determined to follow it through. The pay as advertised was dreadful, but I was going to get a fresh start.

I went down to Kent for the interview and it seemed to be going well. We were getting along splendidly until the chap asked me, 'What was your latest job? What have you just finished?' I told him that I had just come back from America where they had asked me over to help re-stage *Gone With the Wind*. He asked, 'What was your salary?' and when I replied, '$800 a week,' I didn't get another word out of my mouth before I was being thrown out. He thought I couldn't possibly be serious – but I was, I was deadly serious!

Then I started answering all the ads for the Arts Council that appeared in *The Stage*. They were looking for people for jobs such as 'Dance Officer for the South East,' that sort of thing. I thought that sounded fine – I was living in the southeast and I seemed to have the qualifications needed and so I'd go trotting along for these sorts of positions. I would sail through the first interviews and always make the short list for these jobs, but in the end the position would invariably go to somebody with a degree, someone with less practical experience, but with that piece of paper.

Right, I thought, if that's the way they want to play it, so be it. The two shows were running nicely and things looked pretty settled, so I took a deep breath and applied to the Open University. Would I have begun if I'd known exactly how much work would be involved? Probably not. Still, I've never regretted a moment of the six years of hard slog it took to get my Bachelor of Arts. The OU is a remarkable institution. To get your degree you have to amass six full credits. If, like me, you have absolutely no education to count towards your credits, it means starting from square one. You have to do two contrasting Foundation Year courses to get you up to University level. I did one year Arts Foundation and one year Social Sciences. The idea is that you can combine your studies while you work. You have a mass of literature sent to your home, a locally based tutor for emergencies and material broadcast on radio and television. This was before video recorders so the 5 a.m. programmes really were 5 a.m.! They cleverly start you with short assignments of a thousand words or so and fairly soon you're whacking out great long essays. You gain your credit based on set assignments plus a three or four-hour formal examination at the end of each year. Six long grafting years later, at the age of fifty, I was presented with my degree at the Guildford Cathedral along with the great Dame Peggy Ashcroft, who received an honorary one. Was I proud? Just a tad!

Meanwhile, *Oklahoma!* succumbed after a year or so but *Fair Lady* just kept rolling along. After the pre-London tour and a run of nearly

Portrait by Freda Gordon-Hall in my Bachelor of Arts graduation robes.

four years in town, it did a post-London tour and for a final flourish went over to Toronto to play a six-week stint at the Royal Alexandra Theatre. I hadn't been back since playing there as a teenager with the Royal Winnipeg Ballet. We had a great time. My father and brother, of all people, came east to see the show. I introduced them to Dame Anna Neagle and my dear father's life was complete. He had never met anyone so captivating in his life. It was remarkable watching her producing her effect. She had obviously spent a lifetime charming people, but it was totally natural, she was completely without artifice. She was a great lady and worshipped by the company. When I first told her about Peg's Parkinson's she was wonderfully supportive and kind. What I didn't know until after the engagement was over was that she had been diagnosed with it as well. How she disguised the condition all that time was astonishing.

When we got back from Canada, I found that the next show on the Cameron Mackintosh bandwagon had been cancelled. There had been plans to star Elaine Paige in a revival of *South Pacific* with a Broadway baritone, but his dates didn't work out and it had been scuppered. Meanwhile, Cameron was having his office streamlined and modernized. To that end I was taken out to lunch and asked by the two thrusting young modernizers, 'Exactly what did you do in the office while looking after the productions?'

'Well,' I replied, 'when we had to put a replacement into a show, I would arrange an audition, book the theatre, ring round the agents and place an ad in *The Stage*. Then I'd go with an assistant and a pianist and conduct the audition. I would choose somebody, tell him or her they had the job, come back to the office and ring the artist's agent. I would negotiate a salary with the agent and then sit down to type up the contract. I would then arrange a series of rehearsals, first with the understudies, then with the regular cast, where I would direct the newcomer into the show. I would wish him/her luck, see his/her opening night, send flowers for luck and Bob's your Uncle.'

The young men were a trifle subdued. 'You do realise you've been doing about eight people's jobs, don't you?' They were tremendously impressed and admiring and smiled charmingly when they told me that I was sacked. Gillian was already working on a new project, something improbable to do with felines and T.S. Eliot. There was nothing for me to do. Was little Paddy McIntyre going to be out of work after all these years? Was the scrap heap beckoning? Were we all going to starve? Well, no, as it happens.

Peg had always followed the fortunes of the Old Vic after her days there all those years ago. It had been through all sorts of vicissitudes and the latest twist was that the Canadian businessman, Ed Mirvish, had bought it. This was causing all sorts of fuss in the newspapers, with scare stories about the likelihood of it becoming a Bingo Hall or worse. Peg urged me to write; maybe my erstwhile Canadian status would help. I wasn't convinced, but finally overcame my nervousness when I discovered that Ed had appointed Andrew Leigh as his Managing Director over here. Andrew was formerly at the Leicester Haymarket and I had negotiated my *Fair Lady* and *Oklahoma!* contracts with him. I took my courage in both hands and wrote to him asking if there were any managerial posts that I could be considered for. He replied that the management team was all set, but that he hadn't been able to find a House Manager yet. Would I be insulted by the idea of coming in to talk about it?

Insulted? Me? Remember rule 6! Andrew and I had a series of meetings discussing how we'd like our ideal theatre to be run. Weird, strange ideas about friendly box-office staff, welcoming atmosphere, efficiently run bars, all the sorts of things that the West End was notorious for avoiding. It turned out that Andrew had been interviewing for the post for months. The problem seemed to be that the provincial House Managers didn't give the impression they'd be comfortable entertaining Royalty and the like that would be an integral part of the job. The experienced West End people who came, on the other hand, seemed too set in their ways.

After our third meeting Andrew rang and offered me the job. I accepted like a shot. I rang my oldest dancer friend, Barrie Wilkinson, in great excitement to share the news. He was on his way to a theatrical party that same evening. When he announced the news there was a deathly hush. You'd think I had died. The idea of someone giving up the glitz and glamour of the stage for the other side of the curtain was anathema. I looked at the fact that I would have an annual salary for the first time ever, plus the unheard of bonus of four weeks' paid holidays and thought that the scales were pretty evenly balanced. However, bear in mind that I'd never managed anything in my entire life. Even as a child I'd been too busy practising pirouettes to have so much as a lemonade stall in the garden. Now was a perfectly sensible time to PANIC!!

The interior of the theatre at this point was covered in rubble. Ed Mirvish had spent £1,000,000 to buy the Vic and had a wonderful team of theatre architects at work to restore the 1816 building beautifully, but had to agree to spend another £1,000,000 just to shore up the fabric of the building. There were three months to go till the opening. My brief was to sit in the annexe next door and 'staff and stock the building from top to bottom.' It was just like having a beautiful life-sized toy theatre to play with. It would probably have been better if I hadn't been too shy

Three generations of Patrick McIntyres: me, my son, my father, circa 1983.

and too proud to ring up other theatre managers to ask how a theatre should be run, but I just made up my rules as I went along.

I interviewed my lovely staff, many of whom have remained friends to this day, and relied on the kindness of strangers not to rip me off. I had three large bars to stock. Everyone wanted to sell in such a prestigious venue, so I would have a succession of merchants come to me and say things like 'How many cases of champagne would you think you'll get through between deliveries?' Very early on, I found I could act being a House Manager, even if I knew Sweet Fanny Adams about the subject in hand. I'd smile knowingly, lean on my hand and say, 'What would you suggest?' It seemed to work well, but I was convinced that sooner or later I'd have a tap on the shoulder and someone would say, 'You know bugger-all about it' and I'd collapse in a tearful heap and confess all.

I very nearly took to the hills when Andrew informed me a few weeks before opening that the Queen Mother had agreed to come to the Gala opening and 'could you arrange champagne and finger food for her and 1000 guests for that night?' Then, because we were opening with a new Tim Rice musical called *Blondel*, 'Could you arrange a glamorous theatrical opening-night party three days later?' Convinced that the doors would open on that first night and I'd realise that I'd forgotten to order something vital like toilet paper or whatever, even my famous *sang* was a little less *froid* that night. It was a near-run thing. The fitters were still tacking down the stalls carpet as the Queen Mum's chiffon floated through the front doors. It all worked in the end, and she looked lovely sitting in the Royal Box on the Dress Circle level. Sitting in the box opposite her, proud as Punch, was my Dad.

Chapter 19

Choreography and direction…Roy Hudd and Billy Dainty…the Dublin Oklahoma*…guest artiste at Covent Garden…Jack Hulbert and Cicely Courtneidge…Dame Sybil Thorndike at ninety*

BEFORE EMBARKING on the Old Vic years, I'd better tidy up the other bits of career that don't fall neatly into categories such as West End shows, films, television, etc. I've touched on choreography and direction. After the Harlequinade at Leicester, when we came back the following year with *Oklahoma!* Robin Midgley and I collaborated on another piece for the Studio Theatre. Roy Hudd had written a musical entertainment based on the lives of the English songwriters Weston and Lee called *Just a Verse and Chorus.* The two remarkably unremembered composers came together before the First World War and sat in an office every day for the next thirty years churning out almost every British hit you could think of. Everything from 'I'm Henery the Eighth I Am,' 'Joshua, Joshua,' 'With her Head Tucked underneath her Arm,' 'Good-byee, Good-byee,' 'When Father Papered the Parlour,' 'Hello, Hello, Who's your Lady Friend,' right up to 'Knees up Mother Brown.' It was staged as an end of pier stage-within-a-stage show with the characters opening in Pierrot costumes. It was very successful.

The next year we did it again for the Greenwich Theatre and this time Roy played one of the two men himself, opposite Billy Dainty. It was inspired casting. They both used their many years of experience to play the two as cross-talk music hall comedians at a terrific pace with immaculate timing. The following year Robin wasn't available so I directed and staged it myself, this time for the Bromley Theatre followed by a National tour. Roy and Billy were supported by six talented young actor/singer/dancers and it barnstormed round the country getting raves everywhere. I'd pop up here and there to try to keep the two stars in check. It was difficult; one bit in the second act could stretch for twenty minutes of inspired lunacy if they weren't

Opening night speech at my production of Annie Get Your Gun *in Dublin.*

stepped on. The show could have gone on for years. Everyone wanted it back the following year for a longer season. Tragically, however, shortly after the tour ended, Billy Dainty died suddenly from cancer. It was such a devastating blow. He was a lovely, lovely man. Roy kept the sets and costumes in storage for years, but could never bring himself to play it with anyone else. It's never been done since. I've got a video of one of the performances on tour. It's one of my most treasured possessions.

The year after *Oklahoma!* at the Palace ended, I got a call from Dublin. Would I like to come over and direct my own version over there? This was all a trifle odd. Dublin has very little professional musical theatre, but they do have this annual event at the Gaiety Theatre. The Rathgar and Rathmines Musical Society has been going for many years and they book the Gaiety for a week each year, hire a professional orchestra and conductor, a professional director, choreographer and designer and present a full-scale musical to a professional standard, though they themselves are amateur. They rehearse for a month, but only in the evenings or on weekends, so you have your daytimes free, they entertain you royally and pay you a handsome fee in Irish punts. (I suppose it would be in euros nowadays.)

With Albin Pahernik at the Royal Opera House, Covent Garden.

I flew over and the cast were brought in to audition for me, although the principals were fairly settled. In London we had great difficulty in acquiring enough suitable male chorus members, hence my traumas in Bristol. Here, however, at least thirty large, husky men with great soaring voices trooped in. My worries about performance qualities dropped away. The Irish, as well as being naturally talented, are incredibly warm and enthusiastic. Once you make it absolutely clear that you will brook no talking in rehearsals and insist on absolute punctuality, neither of which comes easily to them, they work with real energy. I had a super time. After my opening night speech on stage, I agreed to come back the following year and give them *Annie Get Your Gun*.

Gillian Lynne called in a panic one time. She'd been asked to choreograph the middle balletic act of Sir Michael Tippett's opera *Midsummer Marriage* at Covent Garden and couldn't make head nor tail of the score. Tippett's music is difficult. The same time signature seldom follows from one bar to the next. She desperately wanted me there to count the thing and keep it in my head while she choreographed. She then had a brainwave. She would write mime roles into the ballet for myself and another dancer and call us Presences. We would oversee the action and, more to the point, keep her *au fait* with the score. I simply love the programme that lists me as a Guest Artiste of the Royal Opera House, Covent Garden!

Wendy Toye called with an interesting notion. She was directing a small-scale musical based on the lives of Jack Hulbert and Cicely Courtneidge called *Once More with Music.* They had both been great stars in their time and it was felt that this could be a suitable last hurrah for the elderly couple. Polly James and David Morton would play them as young people and Jack and Cis would gradually take over during the play. Five of us would play all the other people in their lives. Wendy wanted me to assist and look after it on the road after which it might or might not come into town. It sounded fine, but, once rehearsals started, it quickly became apparent that Mr Hulbert's famous charm was reserved entirely for the silver screen. He was an appallingly rude and ungrateful man. He rejected everything that was done to try and help him. He obviously resented having a woman director and treated Wendy shamefully.

One time when we were on the road, Cicely came to me and said that her poor legs were playing up and she was in terrible pain. She asked me to see if Jack would let her enter on his 'revolve' in the darkness rather than having to struggle onto the foot-high riser and wince in front of the audience. I'd barely got the request out when he said, 'No one is on stage during my soliloquy.'

'But Jack, you're in a pin spot, she'll be invisible.'

'No one...' etc. etc.

'But Jack, she's in agony.'

'No one...'

'She's your wife, for Christ's sake!'

Nothing. I gave up.

Despite all the hassle with Mr Hulbert, the show was fun to do and the cast were terrific. I employed my rule 1, 'Fake it.' There was a lot of tap in the show and I can't tap a step to save my life. Here was I, supposedly the choreographic assistant and totally unable to demonstrate the steps. I got very good at casually asking Graham James, a nice guy and a top class tapper to 'just demonstrate that step to the others, would you, sweetheart?' If you're going to fake tapping, make sure your feet make the same moves as the real experts, smile a lot, and above all, unscrew the taps from your shoes so you don't make the wrong noises.

I did the same thing years later when we did the 'London is London' number as tapping guardsmen in bearskin hats in the film musical version of *Good-bye Mr Chips* with Peter O'Toole (again) and Petula Clark. I bet you can't pick out the non-tapping guardsman in the long line of red coats. Actually, it's easy-peasy on a film, as you work to playback and you can make whatever noise you like.

Wendy again. This time it was for a one-off performance at the beautiful Haymarket Theatre to celebrate Dame Sybil Thorndike's ninetieth birthday. Every theatrical Knight and Dame was involved – Olivier, Gielgud, Richardson, Peggy Ashcroft, Judi Dench, Vanessa Redgrave, etc. etc. They did bits from her famous roles and, in one section, played scenes that she had last done anything up to seventy years ago. They would go right up to her cue and she would chime in unfalteringly with her line from the stage box. When the time came for the finale, the stage filled with all the British greats plus every Hollywood star that happened to be in town and quite a few who flew over for the occasion. When the stage was chock-a-block with luminaries, the ninety-year-old Dame Sybil was wheeled on in her chair. Her daughter had been lecturing her backstage, 'Now, Mama, behave yourself. You're not to attempt to stand. Remember what the doctor said.'

Sybil in her wheelchair arrived at front stage centre. The applause was terrific, the cheering stupendous and the whole audience on its feet in a standing ovation. The ninety-year-old Dame threw off her shawl and, like the Phoenix rising from the ashes, slowly grew to her full height and raised her arms aloft in triumph. Her daughter sighed in resignation. It was a magic moment.

There are all sorts of other memories jostling about...the Royal

Command performances…(mostly boring)…the gigs for charity…
(some of them very exciting, including my last ever performance, of
which more later)…the great performances…Olivier's Othello at the
Vic…Judy Garland's Palladium performance as a run-up to her Palace
comeback…Flora Robson in *Ghosts*…Vanessa Redgrave's Rosalind…
many, many more, but we've left the Queen Mother waving graciously
from the Royal Box, so we'd better attend. I am now forty-seven and
about to spend thirteen happy years acting the part of the perfect House
Manager.

Chapter 20

Problems with adapting a 175-year-old theatre…entertaining the Queen, Queen Mother and Prince Philip…so much for royal timekeeping…a plea for photographs

WHEN THE ARCHITECTS refurbished the Old Vic in 1983, they did a splendid job in many respects. Its beautiful horseshoe auditorium was restored to its best period and the front of house made as light and airy as possible, with one grand staircase linking all floors replacing the old segregated system of carpeted stairs between the posh stalls and dress circle, and dank concrete steps leading up to the lower class gallery. Trying to fit all of a modern theatre's facilities into an 1816 building, however, brings fairly intractable problems and decisions regarding priorities and problems of space have to be made. The clash between having enough loos and/or enough bars to get an interval drink remained unsolvable. When I pointed out to the zillionth complainer about queues to the loos that the choice was between turning the entire dress circle bar area into a giant toilet or being able to get his vodka and tonic in comfort, liquor usually won out. Similarly, the restricted view seats in an auditorium designed 175 years ago are going to be a problem. The further round the horseshoe and closer to the stage, the less clear view one has. The cheapness of the price reflects this. I had two extremely irate Australian matrons, however, who came storming down to complain after ten minutes one night. They insisted that such an abomination would never be allowed to be built in fair Australia and demanded to see the original architect!

One decision that proved a great problem for me was that they thought I would be happy working from an office backstage, but obviously if you are Front-of-House Manager you have to be front of house, which meant that I ended up with a cupboard, literally a cupboard, as an office. For thirteen years I had nowhere to entertain very important visitors except my little cubbyhole, which measured six foot by four. It was a maddening problem but all sorts of important people squeezed into that little space and most professed to find it amusing, if nothing else.

Probably the most extraordinary visit, through all those years, was when the Queen appeared. We were doing a very successful revival of *Kiss Me Kate*. Princess Margaret, who came fairly regularly to the theatre, saw it. We were chatting at the interval in my cubbyhole and she said, 'My sister and the Queen Mother would love this. I must see if they can come.' Accordingly, in a week or so I was phoned by the Palace and told that the Queen, the Queen Mother and Prince Philip would like to pay a private visit to the theatre to see the show. The whole point about a private visit, as opposed to a public engagement, is that there is no publicity at all. It's very discreet and the aim is to make it as unobtrusive as possible, with no one knowing ahead of time. I wasn't allowed to tell my staff or anyone else for that matter and the Palace said the measure of our security was that if there were no photographers waiting when they arrived, I would have done a good job.

The night arrived and the very precise arrangements were ready to be followed to the letter. The plan was: the show went up at 7.30 p.m., so at 7.28 p.m. when most of the audience would have gone into the theatre, the royal party would arrive at the front door and I would meet them, take them up to the Dress Circle and guide them to their seats in the middle of the front row. This wasn't a display – they weren't going to sit in the Royal Box, they were just going to slip into real seats amongst the audience in the middle of the first row of the Dress Circle. They would get to their seats just as the house lights were going down. When they sat down, the conductor would take this as his cue to start the show. Everything was all arranged on that basis.

Come the night, I was standing at the raised section at the back of the entrance foyer at approximately 7.15 p.m. getting ready to meet and greet. The foyer was packed. It was a full house and people were milling around trying to pick up their tickets or find friends. Looking down and across the heads of the throng, I suddenly noticed three little figures standing on the front steps by the doors, the Queen, the Queen Mother and Prince Philip, having been dumped there – well, dropped there – by their driver. Meanwhile, their attendant had gone back to the car, as he had forgotten the martini shaker they were planning to use for their interval drinks, and had to retrieve it. There they were, having been dropped thirteen minutes early. So much for the fabled Royal precision with timing! I tried to make my way through the crowd to meet them and the General Manager, Andrew Leigh, tried to fight his way through from the other side of the foyer. Meanwhile people were going by with that 'don't be silly, it can't be' look on their faces as they passed the royal party. As I made my way towards them I tried to decide what to do. I couldn't squeeze them all into my little office, so Andrew and I took them up to the Dress Circle bar and hoped that somehow the audience would sit down quickly and I could take them in. I couldn't usher them in beforehand because the show would start without an audience. There was no way I could get to the conductor to give him his revised cue.

For those fifteen minutes, the Queen and I (I seemed to get the Queen to chat to while Andrew had the Queen Mother and Prince Philip) chatted of this and that and Her Majesty said, 'It was amazing. We just whizzed over Waterloo Bridge, there was no traffic at all tonight!' We were jammed into a crowded and noisy bar and the situation seemed totally surreal. A patron wrote a very nice article for Punch Magazine the next week telling how his wife did the nose trick with her drink when she realised that the woman pressed against her left shoulder was her Sovereign. Finally the Queen said, 'I really would like to sit down now.' To reply, 'Well, you can't, so there' wasn't really an option. It was still a bit early but I had been doing a lot of eyebrow acting to my staff to get the audience in as quickly as they could. Most of them had settled, so I led them to their seats and got the show up. There was one tiny contretemps on the way when one poor lady decided to dash to the ladies before curtain up and came face to face with Her Majesty at the door of the Circle. She gave a startled shriek, dropped a quick curtsey and ran.

I'd had strict instructions about the martinis for the interval. The shaker was to go into the freezer along with the glasses to be used. At the last minute you take the martini shaker and the glasses, plus a bucket of ice, to the Stage Box where we were to entertain them. The Queen Mother's ritual was to pour the martinis herself and enquire, 'Ice and lemon, anyone?' It was all set up and all that part went smoothly. Afterwards, my staff had a chance to taste the remains of the martinis and they were very, very strong – straight gin basically. After the interval all bets were off, of course, because the whole audience had seen who was there. When I brought them back from the Box to their seats again, the audience spontaneously turned to face the Royal Party and gave them a nice round of applause. It was a charming gesture. The Queen Mother leaned over to the Queen and asked if they should stand and wave. The Queen hissed, 'No, Mother, sit down' and we got the second act up.

Getting them out at the end was a bit difficult because we had to cordon off the route from down the main staircase to the front door. We put out the stanchions and velvet ropes so that the audience could be on one side and watch them come down while we got them out of the front door. At the end of the performance, Her Majesty and I came down the stairs together and because I had been so avid and meticulous in my security arrangements, there is not one picture of me with the Queen. None of my staff knew anything about it until the night in question and were strictly forbidden cameras in any case. Meanwhile, there must be hundreds of pictures of us all over America and Japan, because the tourists were all busily snapping away like mad. If there is anyone abroad who remembers the night, please send me a copy!

Chapter 21

A theatrical non-person…the Mirvish family run the Vic…Marcel Marceau and things that go bump in the night…entertaining Barbara Bush and the G7 ladies…Downing Street reception

YOU CAN GET so involved in the day-to-day hassles of front of house life – keeping the punters happy, trying to ensure profits from your bar and ice cream sales, making sure you have quality part-time staff, coping with floods in the downstairs bar or leaks from the nineteenth century roof, or even entertaining glamorous guests – that you can forget the main function of the place, putting on shows. It takes a little time to realise, however, that once you make that shift to the other side of the curtain, you are a theatrical non-person. Despite my thirty-five years of experience performing and/or directing in the business, during my entire thirteen years at the Vic, there was never a single instance when my opinion was sought as to what should or should not be performed.

That wouldn't matter so much if you weren't left holding the can. If a production is truly terrible, the producer and director will be long gone and you're the one with the glazed expression and the dinner jacket left trying to appease the enraged patrons. I don't know where the reputation of the English being reluctant to complain came from. In my experience they're only too happy to harangue endlessly and ad nauseum. If it's about a faulty dryer in the loo, fine, you hold up your hands and accept full responsibility. If it's about Deborah Kerr forgetting every line in *The Corn is Green*, there's very little you personally can do about it.

The Mirvish family had bought the Old Vic having had great success in running the Royal Alexandra Theatre in Toronto. They used a subscription system, where patrons bought tickets for a whole season of plays running for a fixed number of weeks each. They had built up an element of trust through the years, so announcements such as 'among the stars appearing this season' or 'some of the musicals to be announced later' etc. were accepted at face value. They could sell up to 90 per cent of their seats up front before the season started and the punters were stoical and forgiving when 'the stars' turned out to be less luminous that they had hoped.

London turned out to be a trickier proposition. For one thing there is far greater competition, with over forty West End theatres vying for trade every evening. The other major problem is the floating population of tourists who won't be in town for the next play but one and only want to see what's available the week they're here. Crucially, however, not enough regular home-grown theatregoers would commit themselves for a particular Monday, say, the following July, however tempting the offer is in September. The result was a take-up of subscriptions less than would guarantee financial success. This wouldn't be of concern if each individual play was successful and dragged in the casual punter, but hit or miss, they each had to run their allotted six weeks to satisfy the subscribers who *had* booked ahead for a particular night. That meant having to close some shows when they were still selling out and having the dogs limp along for their full-allotted six weeks. There's nothing worse than having to repeat a failure night after night to empty houses.

There were plenty of hits as well, of course, although sometimes they brought problems of their own. The computer glitch that double booked an entire coach party, for instance, to an already sold-out house, the star refusing to begin the second act until a punter taking an illegal photograph in the first act finale has had the film confiscated, or even the mime artist who wanted me to have the Lord Mayor's Show cancelled.

This latter instance was the culmination of a series of irritations and frustrations in dealing with the giant ego of Marcel Marceau. When it was announced that M. Marceau was to give one last series of performances at the Old Vic before his retirement, everyone was excited. Ticket sales were brisk and we looked forward to a nice run of sell-out houses. Before he opened, however, his entourage arrived with items we were to sell at our little front-of-house outlet. Ours was a very modest affair; we had neither the space nor the storage to cope with more than the usual T-shirt and programme sales. M. Marceau fancied himself as a serious painter, however, and insisted we display his large daubs to 'sell' for hundreds of pounds, as well as large, expensive, china dolls of himself as 'Bip.' Despite our advice that our patrons did not come to the theatre expecting to part with large sums for these sorts of items and have to cart them off to dinner afterwards, nothing would dissuade him.

Every night for the six-week run, he would send someone to get the sales figures and every night we'd say 'Rien.' It was embarrassing, but we coped. The run itself went smoothly with very satisfactory houses until we came to the very last night. He had made a big thing about this being possibly his last performance ever and people had come from all over the country, from the continent, and over from America to see the show. (The fact that he almost immediately embarked on yet another 'farewell' tour is neither here nor there). My staff and I shoehorned the audience into every available crevice in the auditorium and I gave the cue for the show to start.

We settled back for a well-earned cup of cheer when fifteen minutes into the show we heard noises coming from the auditorium. Noises, from a mime show? We rushed in to find an empty stage and an extremely puzzled audience. Apparently the star had appeared, done his first piece, made a show of exasperation (who better?) and had stalked off stage. I ran backstage to find him ranting and raving, in French, about some sort of noise and refusing to go back on stage. ('Jamais, jamais!!') I sent for Andrew, the General Manager, whose French was better than mine, to see if he could make sense of the situation. Meanwhile, the natives in the audience were getting restless and a decision would have to be made soon.

It finally transpired that M. had gone on stage and heard noises that he thought were caused by his crew packing up early to get away quickly on his last night. When he was persuaded that this wasn't the case, he still insisted that something was making a noise that wasn't there in previous performances. I suddenly realized that it was the Saturday of the Lord Mayor's Show. There is an annual fireworks display on the Thames and he must have heard distant bangs and thumps from that. 'Ring up and tell them to cancel!' he shrieked. When that wasn't possible, he finally settled for me going on stage and grovelling to get the patrons back on his side. He primed me with the speech. I was to explain that this 'great artiste' was 'ultra-sensitive' to disturbance and had left the stage 'with a heavy heart.' He didn't want to disappoint 'his loving and loyal fans', however, and if they would give him time to recover from 'his emotional turmoil,' he would shortly return. I went out and did my bit, just managing to avoid throwing up, given my overload of greasy charm. The slow handclapping and booing settled down, there was a pause and the great man reappeared to a standing ovation. Did he thank me, or apologise for being a Gallic prat? Don't be daft!

In between the various ventures into subscription systems, the one-off musicals that had their own natural runs were probably the most successful ventures. I've mentioned *Kiss Me Kate* that brought in the Royal Family. Among others, a distinguished production of *Carmen Jones* did very well, as did Bernstein's *Candide* with the enchanting Patricia Routledge.

When the G7 conference was held in London, Downing Street called to ask me if I would entertain Barbara Bush, Norma Major and thirty other high-powered ladies from the various countries to a performance and supper at the Old Vic. We were playing *Carmen Jones* at the time. This was felt to be a suitable show for them and all was arranged. It turned out to be very lively evening, but the order of protocol between all these ladies – Ambassadors' wives, Presidents' wives, etc. – was very tricky.

The black limos arrived one by one in Waterloo Road. First to arrive was Mrs Major who established herself at the bottom of the stairs in the Pit Bar to greet her guests after I had met them at the top and brought them down to her. The long line of cars climaxed with Mrs Bush, whose limo was followed by a completely equipped and staffed Military Ambulance that stayed parked outside the theatre all evening. I never did figure out why; it wasn't her finger on the nuclear button after all. So far so good. Everyone had arrived and was munching contentedly on canapés and sipping Buck's Fizz. Now to get them up into the auditorium. As there's no centre aisle at the Vic, I had the bright idea of arranging them in protocol school crocodiles, marching them up the side aisles and have them meet in the middle. I took Mrs Bush and fifteen ladies in order of precedence, my assistant did the same with Mrs Major and her lot and got them organised. Getting them to abandon their Buck's Fizz and their gossip to get into line wasn't easy,

Entertaining Barbara Bush at the Old Vic.

but I adopted my best St. Trinian's Headmistress manner, clapped my hands, 'Now then, ladies!!' and they meekly fell into line. We reversed the procedure at the interval and all was well.

The consequence of all this was rather fun. The Majors invited me to 10 Downing Street for a reception a few weeks later. That was a fascinating evening. It was wonderful to see inside Downing Street and go up those stairs with all the former Prime Ministers' portraits on the wall. Once inside, the house opens up like Dr Who's Tardis. It's far bigger inside than the impression given from the exterior. We were in a beautiful reception room upstairs. It was an informal occasion to thank a number of people who had helped to make the G7 conference go smoothly. In those days, of course, there were no protesters – the general notion was that these conferences were rather a good thing. I suppose Seattle changed all that. It was certainly a good thing as far as I was concerned – I had a lovely time.

Chapter 22

*Peg's decline…managing the symptoms…down to the seaside…the
true horrors of the disease…Trivial Pursuit…a broken heart*

ALL THE PRECEDING chapters were written in no time flat. No matter
how busy I've been with other work, I've had no difficulty in
whipping off a chapter or so in an evening. I've enjoyed the process.
After resisting the well-meaning naggers urging me to get my 'unusual'
life down on paper for years, once started I was off to the races. Each
episode seemed to fall into place in a logical order and I've had a great
time remembering each slice of my life. This one is difficult, however. I
feel I must tell about Peg's decline and have been putting it off for
weeks. It's hard to revisit the pain, but I owe it to a remarkable lady to
try. Here goes.

When I accepted the Old Vic job, Peg had been coping with the
beginnings of Parkinson's for nearly four years. The main symptoms in
the early stages for her (each case varies enormously) were the tremor
in her left hand along with the curious involuntary quickening of steps
resulting in a fall; or the exact reverse, a freezing to the spot and being
unable to move forward at all. The recent discovery of L-dopa was
hailed as a major breakthrough in treating the disease and did, indeed,
help enormously in the beginning. A half-tablet, taken every four hours,
would miraculously stop the tremor and free the ability to control
walking.

I negotiated my contract to do a full week's work in three and a half
days at the theatre so I'd be home every other day with her and we
coped very well. Before long, however, a half-tablet wasn't enough and
the symptoms grew more virulent. We'd crank up the dosage to keep up
but ran into the limitations of the new drug. I'm sure the approach is
much more scientific nowadays but, back then, you were left to your
own devices to experiment with the amount to take, the problem being
that an overdose of the drug produces the exact same symptoms as the

disease itself, so you spend your life trying to decide if you've given too much or too little while poor Peg is shaking like a wet dog and, unbelievably, still managing to remain cheerful.

In the main, we were managing a routine that kept the worst of the physical limitations at bay. Peg was still managing to cook and look after the house with a bit of help and to take her daily walks. One night, however, I came home from the theatre to find that she'd buttered a raffia place mat for my supper. It was a truly shocking moment. Nothing had prepared us for the ghastly fact that it was going to attack her mind as well. Nothing. Her beautiful, intelligent, enquiring mind was going to be reduced to nothing. By the end she couldn't read, write, or even watch television. Meanwhile, she didn't go off into a happy world of her own, as some Alzheimer sufferers seem to do. She would do something extraordinary and then come back to normal for a while and find it difficult to believe the evidence of her actions. When she did comprehend the truth, she *knew* she was losing her mind. I think that's probably the cruellest blow of all.

We had wonderful friends and neighbours who would come in at regular intervals to make sure Peg took her pills. She could never remember if she had taken the last lot. When she was regular, we would have stretches of comparative normality contrasted with moments of high tragedy or pure farce. It became evident that we'd have to give up the little house, however. Peg couldn't make the stairs easily and it became too dangerous for her to walk in the woods by herself. One memorable night the poor love had a violent attack of diarrhoea, tried to go down the hall to the bathroom, lost control of her walking and fell at the head of the stairs. I tried to raise her up but, not to put too fine a point on it, kept slipping in the shit and falling down with her. The space was too narrow to get any leverage. After pushing and pulling and sliding in the muck for what seemed like hours, I managed to get us both into the tub and sluice us down with the shower hose. Peg stood passively and meekly allowed herself to be hosed down. Up till then she hadn't been making any sense but I caught her eye and could tell that suddenly her mind had returned, however fleetingly. She looked at me, sized up the situation and started to laugh. She started me off and the two of us stood there covered in shit and laughed and laughed and cried and cried.

David was married by this time and he and his wife were working as solicitors in Brighton. When we went down to visit them, I fell in love with the seaside and the beautiful Regency architecture and thought that the flatness of the promenade would be perfect for Peg's exercise. We sold the little house and bought a huge ground floor flat in Palmeira Square in Hove. There were some who felt that the 27-foot drawing room, marble fireplaces and crystal chandeliers were a bit above our station. As my friend Barrie so elegantly put it, 'It isn't a flat, it's a fucking Embassy.'

We settled in, nevertheless, and managed to have some nice walks along the front. As long as Peg clung to my arm and rested every once in a while, the sea air seemed to invigorate her and we had very few accidents. Her mind was rapidly failing, however. We couldn't rely on friends to come in every few hours, but our doctor put us in touch with the Independent Living Fund. This is (or was, I don't know if it still exists) a government-funded organization to help carers keep their jobs and their sanity as long as possible. It helped pay for wonderful women to come in and tackle whatever was needed while I was away at work. At first they would stay until she had settled down for the night, but after I had come home one night to find that Peg had got up, turned on all the taps in the flat and then wandered out in her nightgown, clutching a selection of photographs, and hailed a cab to take her to Monck Street, our old address in Winnipeg, it was obvious she couldn't be left alone for a second. On this occasion the kindly cabbie had taken her to the local police station and I went there to collect her. I got her home and settled her in bed. At three in the morning we had a frantic call from the chap who owned the flat below us. He'd come home to find his sitting room flooded and water still coming through the ceiling rose of his light fixture.

The horrors of the next eighteen months were hard to bear. Some effects were truly weird. Peg would see two of me, the real me and an imaginary me sitting in another chair. She would address her conversation to the other me and nothing would persuade her that I was the real me. She was convinced that I was having passionate affairs with those wonderful patient women who were looking after her and treated them dreadfully. She would sit in our huge elegant drawing room and rail and rage for hours about how I had dragged her into this tiny hovel. Turning against loved ones is fairly common in this situation, but desperately hard to cope with. At one point the doctors decided I needed respite and arranged to take her into hospital for a couple of weeks. It lasted two days. They called me after the first night to say that she'd tried to escape twice in her nightgown and bare feet and had fought with the nurses. I sat with her the rest of the day and she seemed a bit calmer. The children went to see her the next morning and were devastated when she didn't recognise them at all. I went in and realised that she'd caused them more problems during the night and that they'd doped her to the eyeballs to keep her quiet. I dressed her and brought her straight back home. So much for respite.

By what would turn out to be her last Christmas Peg was in a shocking state. She had physically shrunk and mentally withdrawn and wouldn't cooperate with any of the family celebrations. This was hard as she'd always been so passionate about family togetherness. We were all there and tried to pretend that everything was normal. We couldn't persuade her to come to the dinner table, however. She sat in a corner and glowered while we got on with carving the turkey and blazing the pudding. Somehow we got through the meal and, as this was when Trivial Pursuit was all the rage, cleared the table and set out the game. I made one last appeal to Peg to come and join us. I managed to get her up and persuaded her over to the table. Then the most extraordinary thing happened. We started the game and Peg answered every single Trivial Pursuit question that came up. It didn't matter what category, the question would be asked and she would have the answer. Both before and immediately after the game she was virtually catatonic, but during it her old intelligence blazed away like a shooting star.

By mid-summer of 1990 our thirty-third wedding anniversary was due. For some reason I decided we needed a big party. If Peg had a bad day, the family could work out a rota to cope with her, but you never knew. I invited all sorts of people down from London, some I hadn't seen for ages. The day was perfect, one of those amazing late June English sunshine days. The roses in the back garden were at their best and Peg was in her element. She came out to the garden on my arm and chatted away to the guests with all her old charm. I'm not convinced she actually recognised any of them, but she was playing the gracious hostess to the manner born. It was a lovely day.

Three days later I was getting her organised in the morning before handing her over to the helpers and going to work. I'd got her sitting on the edge of the bed and given her the first pills of the day to hold. I went into the bathroom for her water, heard a clunk and came back to find that she had fallen to the floor. She was breathing with a terrible rattling noise and I realised immediately that this was the end. The emergency services came very quickly and worked very hard but to no avail. I called the children who came and were a great support. They all agreed with me that this was a wonderful release for poor Peg. Indeed, Hilary remarked that the mother she had known had died a good three years before. I was so pleased that I had been there when it happened.

It turned out that the Parkinson's had no bearing on her death. There's a heart condition where the tissues surrounding the heart get progressively thinner and thinner without presenting any symptoms. Eventually they are too thin to support the beating heart and simply burst. This is what happened to poor Peg. My beloved wife died, quite literally, of a broken heart.

Chapter 23

*Charity gigs…Royal Command…Miss Diana Ross…Dot Cotton
and Ethel…on Broadway with Liza Minnelli et al…my last stage
appearance*

My thirteen years at the Old Vic were sufficiently engrossing to help keep me balanced during Peg's sickness as well as forcing me to push on once she'd gone. I kept the three and a half day week from force of habit, although the fourteen-hour days did get tiresome after a while. I wasn't totally divorced from the performance side of the business, however.

Numbers like the 'Ascot Gavotte' and 'Get me to the Church' from *My Fair Lady* were in fairly constant demand for charity performances and the like. A few times a year I'd get requests to round up the old cast and recreate one or other of the numbers. These always came with mixed emotions. It was wonderful to have reunions with people you'd played together so long with, but all too often they were memorial performances for departed friends. Depending on the time I could afford to get off from the Vic, I would either just direct and rehearse the numbers or amuse myself by appearing in them myself.

One of the 'Gavotte' outings was for a Royal Command Performance. It was decided to honour Cameron Mackintosh and the whole first act was taken up with excerpts from his shows: *Cats*, *Phantom of the Opera*, *Les Miserables*, *Fair Lady*, *Song and Dance* etc. etc. All the principal players who'd been in them came back for this one night, so the cast was practically the entire West End musical theatre establishment.

The second act had the usual variety of acts culminating in an appearance by Miss Diana Ross. These things are always rehearsed separately and thrown together on the camera call on the Sunday. This is the only time the artists can get to see each other's performances. It's normally a jolly occasion with people dashing out front to catch the camera rehearsal of their favourites. This time was a bit different. After everyone else had blocked his or her numbers, it was announced on the tannoy that Miss Ross would be rehearsing after the break. It was requested that we should all sit in the Dress Circle to watch her and leave the stalls free for the cameras. Fine.

We all came back from the break and settled down in the Circle. Miss Ross's band was in place at the back of the stage, her high stool was set down front in a spotlight. There was a pause, however, and raised voices could be heard backstage. It developed that the lady objected to the rest of the cast watching her rehearse. 'I'm not going to perform for that lot!' Considering that 'that lot' were the biggest stars of the British theatre, it seemed a tad churlish. In the event she stomped onstage, dragged her stool to the back of the stage and went through her act in sotto voce. She sat facing her band with her back to the audience and never turned round. Meanwhile the spotlight went through her pre-arranged moves without her. It looked like the death of Pavlova.

Come the evening during the live show, we got to the first act finale. This consisted of a gradual build up on stage of the entire cast doing the big flag-waving number from *Les Miz*. The huge company lined up from the wings and all the way down the dressing room corridor. I was last in line, with a nervous Cameron clutching my hand. The idea was that I would smuggle him on to back centre stage, the cast would part like the Red Sea and he would stroll forward in his kilt to take his applause. The number was building to a crescendo and we were psyching ourselves up for our entrance when the stage door burst open. Two of Ms Ross's heavies appeared and announced that her limo was approaching and we would have to clear the corridor. Apparently she insists that no one is in the corridor as she makes her way from stage door to dressing-room. The heavies, however, had not met the British luvvie in full cry before. Well, 'tough shit, baby'…'send the cow round the block'…these and a few other choice epithets, delivered in a fierce backstage hiss, sent them retreating until we had made our entrance.

We did another performance of the 'Gavotte' for Ray Cook's memorial. He was the wonderful musical director who'd come over from Australia to conduct many of the West End shows I'd appeared in. This time I had to rehearse 'Dot Cotton' and 'Ethel' from the soap opera *EastEnders* into the number. The idea this time was that they'd be unrecognisable in the period costumes and enormous hats until they turned front at the end and delivered Eliza's line 'Move your blooming arse!' Like so many bright ideas, however, this one failed to take in the actors' basic character. There was absolutely no way those two super ladies were not going to find a way to be recognised IMMEDIATELY and milk the number for laughs all the way through. Of course, we all played the game. I drilled them in the moves. They rehearsed in deadly earnest. We all knew, though, that come the performance it would be a whole new ball-game. Normally this sort of thing can drive you crazy, but when you have vastly experienced and talented character actors like those two for a one-off performance, you keep your head down.

When Alan J. Lerner died of lung cancer in 1986, his widow Liz Robertson organised two extraordinary evenings in his memory over the next few years to aid lung cancer charities. The first was held at Drury Lane and featured wonderful artists who had been associated with his music through the years along with a few happy surprises. One very nice moment had the three actors who had played Freddie Eynsford-Hill in the London run sing 'On the Street where you Live' in canon and then be joined by a fourth, one Placido Domingo, for the final chorus. Magic. We provided our 'Ascot Gavotte' (straight this time) and it was a lovely emotional evening.

The second evening, however, was on a monumental scale. It was held at the New York State Theatre in Lincoln Centre on Broadway. It starred, among others, Liza Minnelli, Julie Andrews, Jane Powell, Rudolph Nureyev, Van Johnson, Douglas Fairbanks Jr., Georgia Brown and every current star on Broadway. The organisers were determined to have something from Alan's last *Fair Lady* production, so they asked three of us to go over and perform the 'Little Bit of Luck' trio. Accordingly, Peter Baylis, the London 'Alfie Doolittle', Peter Durkin, who had also been in the show and myself jetted over for a magical five days. Richard Branson's contribution was to fly us over Upper Class; we were met by a white limo at JFK and taken to a Park Lane hotel. We were given an American chorus to train up to be Cockney background characters and treated like royalty.

The American punters shelled out $25,000 for five tickets that got them their seats and supper for six in the Grand Foyer afterwards. One of us filled the sixth place. Some lucky punters got Ms Minnelli or the equivalent. Other poor sods got me. You can't win them all! I shared a

Rehearsing 'Little Bit of Luck' with Peter Baylis and Peter Durkin for my last ever stage appearance on Broadway.

dressing-room with Lee Roy Reames, a terrific young Broadway dancer who was doing 'How could you believe me when I said I loved you when you know I've been a liar all my life?' with Jane Powell. Alan had written the number for Miss Powell and Fred Astaire for the movie *Royal Wedding* in 1958. They played a clip of it before she came on and, astonishingly, she looked better forty years on. I sat beside her in the Green Room watching the monitor during the show and there were no signs of artificiality at all. They recreated the number exactly and Lee Roy couldn't get over her energy. He was in his twenties and found the going tough while she in her sixties (??) barely worked up a sweat. He finally challenged her on the subject. She smiled sweetly and said, 'In MGM we were trained never to sweat no matter what. We were only allowed to glow!'

Funny to think that the beautiful new theatre stands on the site of my $50 per week apartment hotel of the 1950s. It's a stunning building, seating 2,000. In memory of Alan and the original Ascot costume designs, the ladies were asked to wear black and white and diamonds, the men black tie. The interior is red plush and gold. As I stood in the prompt corner waiting for my entrance, you could peek out front and the effect was dazzling. Our cue came. Kitty Carlisle Hart, widow of the great Moss Hart, introduced us. 'And now, all the way from England…' I suddenly realised something was very odd. I had absolutely no nerves whatsoever. I thought, 'If I can't get even the slightest bit worked up about going on and singing a trio in this place with this sort of cast, it's time to give up performing.' It's not that I didn't have a terrific time; I did. The cast party in the pub afterwards was sensational. 'Go on, Liza, give us a song.'…The more I thought about it, however, the more sense it made. That is why October 23 1989 marks my last performance on stage. I was fifty-three.

Chapter 24

*Back to reality…the Jonathan Miller season…Sir John Gielgud's
seventy-fifth…Christopher Reeve…Paul Newman…stars, royalty
and those close to them*

Back in the real world, I climbed once again into my dinner jacket and took charge of the Vic again. There was one very funny after-note from the adventure a few weeks later. The lovely actress Susan Wooldridge came to see a performance one evening. I had admired her work since she had starred in *The Jewel in the Crown* on television. Her brother, Hugh, had directed the Broadway charity gig and she'd gone over to give support. On this particular night I was behind the foyer counter helping my staff give out pre-paid tickets. Miss Wooldridge was making her way through the throng towards the counter, spotted me, did a double take and shrieked, 'Good God, the last time I saw you, you were starring on Broadway!!' That caused a few heads to turn, I can tell you. I blushed prettily, shuffled my feet and gave my 'aw, shucks' Jimmy Stewart impression.

There were the usual ups and downs with play choices. The Mirvishes made a very brave decision one year to hand the season over to Jonathan Miller. The brilliant Dr Miller had carved a very distinguished career for himself since the heady days of *Beyond the Fringe*. He was a wonderful pundit on the history of theatre on television and managed to make the most erudite academic approaches to the subject accessible and entertaining. His imaginative forays into direction were widely admired, particularly in opera. His appointment was welcomed both by press and public. He then announced a season of semi-forgotten eighteenth and nineteenth century plays. A few alarm bells started to ring. He had dug out some real gems, however. *The Liar*, starring Alex Jennings, currently playing Prof. Higgins in the latest revival of *Fair Lady* was just sensational. It got rave reviews, as did several other plays. Some, however, demonstrated perfectly clearly why they had been forgotten. Brecht had done one of them, *The Tutor*, with his Berliner Ensemble. There was great excitement when Dr Miller brought over Brecht's assistant director from Berlin. However, she then proceeded to direct the already turgid piece at such a snail's pace that the poor audience was begging for mercy after the first scene.

The season lurched on, however, and it was generally felt that the successes outweighed the outright failures and even they had some distinguishing features. The last productions of the season were to prove too much, however, even for the long-suffering Mirvishes. There was to be a production of *Lulu* alternating with a modern German play. A very distinguished cast was signed to play in both. Then it was announced that the elaborate set would mean ripping out the stall seats back to row H. When the theatre accountant gently pointed out that the plays would have to play to 110 per cent capacity merely to break even, that was it. The Mirvishes cancelled the shows, paid off the actors and looked around for a replacement.

They soon found one. Derek Jacobi was touring the provinces in a production of *Kean*. It was a lovely old potboiler with a meaty leading part and Mr Jacobi was more than happy to extend his season with a run at the Old Vic. I was standing in the foyer at the interval on its opening night. Before the applause had died down, a clearly furious Jonathan Miller stormed out of the stalls. 'If that's the sort of bloody rubbish the British public wants,' he raged, 'they can bloody well have it' and he swept off into the night. The problem is, Dr Miller, they mostly do.

On my side of the curtain we amused ourselves by dreaming up various schemes to hire out the beautiful areas for entertaining. A few ended in tears, such as the late night rock discos in the bars that drove our neighbours frantic, but daytime book launches and receptions proved very popular. My favourite party was one organized for Sir John Gielgud's seventy-fifth birthday. Everyone from the profession was there to pay tribute. He sat on stage while the speeches were made and my job was to cue Christopher Reeve to bring the cake on. Mr Reeve was in town to make the second Superman movie and at the height of his fame. It was felt that his bounding on with the birthday cake would amuse Sir John. The problem was that, at the critical moment, Mr

Reeve froze. We were standing in the wings when he suddenly said, 'This is the most famous stage in the world and sitting on it is probably the best actor in the world. I can't possibly go out there. I'm just a lousy movie star!'

'Nonsense,' I said, 'he'll love it' and gave him a shove. What a nice, charming man he is. His accident a few years later was tragic and poignant.

When the ceremony was over and everyone had trooped out to the bars for drinks, Sir John asked if we could sit quietly for a minute before facing the throng. There then followed one of those occasions when you long for a tape recorder. He and I sat on the steps leading down from the stage while he looked around at the theatre where he'd had all those triumphs as a very young man. He told fascinating stories about the pre-war Old Vic, not necessarily about performances, but practicalities such as the perennial lack of money, dearth of dressing-room space, the rough and ready audiences who would always catalogue your faults in full voice from the gallery but who, once won over, were fiercely loyal. It was a magic ten minutes and a treasured memory.

Probably the next most memorable encounter was with another great actor, but from an entirely different tradition, Mr Paul Newman. The author, Tom Stoppard, brought Mr Newman and his wife Joanne Woodward to the theatre to see the Greek tragedy, *Medea*. When they arrived before the show, Ms Woodward asked if she could sit by herself on the end of a row as she wasn't feeling well and was suffering from jet lag having just flown in from LA. Sure enough, half-way through the act, she came out, very pale, and we arranged a car to take her back to the hotel. Mr Newman was fine, however. At the end of the play, Mr Stoppard brought him front of house and asked if I could look after him while he went backstage for a while. As we stood and chatted in the foyer, the audience were filing by and, of course, checking out Mr Newman. The nice thing about an English audience is that they would never dream of bothering someone like that and everything was proceeding peacefully. Suddenly, however, an American matron of uncertain years came up to us and demanded his autograph. Paul Newman, with great courtesy and charm, apologized and explained to the woman that he never gave autographs. It was just something he never had done. She took great exception to this and became very loud and boorish. 'Who do you think you are? Where would you be without us?' etc. Things were getting a bit out of hand, so I reached behind me for the door handle of my office, opened the little door, grabbed Mr Newman's arm and whisked him backwards into the room. A ruefully grateful movie star then settled down for a nice gossip. (And yes, his eyes are really that blue.) He's a genuinely nice, thoughtful man. The last thing I remember him saying before Tom Stoppard came to collect him was, referring to the play, 'Oooh, those Greeks really knew how to do it, didn't they?'

There were so many others, some surprising you with their differences in real life, some confirming one's initial impression. The lovely Claudette Colbert as a very elderly lady, for instance, beautifully dressed in a Chanel suit, still with the fringe and short bob and big dark eyes, walking slowly but elegantly on the arms of two handsome young men. For a moment the charm and style of 1940s Hollywood was alive and well. Faye Dunaway, whose reputation is a bit difficult, confounding her critics by taking the trouble to rifle through her programme before the show so as to thank me *by name* for her interval drinks. Now that's classy!

Prince and Princess Michael of Kent came to see an interesting play called *Master Class*. It was about how Stalin treated the great Russian composers during his era. The Prince looks, of course, startlingly like his relative, the last Czar of Russia. At the interval he told me how, as a young man, he'd been sent to Paris to learn Russian from the White Russian émigrés. He was fascinating, describing these people sitting ramrod straight in their Paris salons, still living as if in the court of St Petersburg, gravely following the strictest protocol, but like grey, quiet, almost translucent ghosts.

One evening a remarkably chic lady came to the theatre with a small party. She was dressed very fashionably in understated black with some very good diamonds. Her legs were excellent and she had great style and presence. One of the men in her party came to the counter and asked for 'the tickets for Mrs Parker Bowles, please'. Whether she is genuinely not photogenic or whether the press scrambled around to print the worst possible pictures of her to please their favourite, Princess Diana, is a moot point, but she bears no resemblance to her

The famous tiny office.

accepted image. I was pleased to see her in the flesh, as I've always
considered that she is the one person in the whole sorry saga that has
behaved with impeccable dignity throughout.

Chapter 25

Approaching retirement…the big party…another career beckons…
the tortoiseshell cat and I…move to a granny flat…Senior Assessor
Trinity College

As I got within shouting distance of my sixtieth birthday, thoughts of retirement kept surfacing. I'd worked thirteen years at the Old Vic and, though still finding it enjoyable and stimulating, there was certainly an element of routine creeping in. One night a chap called Matt Winston came to the theatre. He'd been in the Winnipeg ballet company when I was a child and had since lived over here in the UK for many years. 'Do you realise,' I remarked to him, 'that it's been fifty years since my first performance on stage in *Pleasure Cruise*?'

'I know,' he replied dryly, 'I played your father!'

That chance encounter started me planning the big retirement party. I like symmetry and neatness, and the idea of a big celebration to mark fifty years in the business, my sixtieth birthday and the announcement of my retirement in one fell swoop had great appeal. The planning took months. Andrew Leigh promised me the theatre for a Sunday in June. The invitations went out to the colonies for far-flung relatives and colleagues to make plans to holiday in London that summer. Ads went into *The Stage* newspaper for old friends to get in touch. Old address books were combed for telephone numbers. Once acceptances from abroad were confirmed, I snapped up all the available short-rent apartments from an estate agent down on the coast. Hire cars and coaches were booked, musicians were hired and enough booze to float London was negotiated at a cut rate from my faithful suppliers.

The day dawned. It was perfect weather. All my Canadian relatives who had already been over for a couple of weeks had their prejudices shattered when not a drop of rain fell during their entire visit. We drove up to London in our finery. My wonderful sister, Marguerite, was with me along with a myriad of cousins and nieces and children and grandchildren. The theatre looked stunning. I'd opened the Dress Circle bar area as well as the Lilian Baylis Circle above it so that people could circulate up and down the grand staircase (and never be too far away from a drink). About 350 friends and relatives turned up in the end. We started at three in the afternoon with drinks and canapés, went into the theatre proper for the formalities about five o'clock, back out for desserts and, of course, more drinks, and carried on till about eleven in the evening. It was a lovely, lovely day.

My assistant manager, Ned Seago, had arranged the formal bit on stage in the middle of the proceedings so as to provide me with some surprises. We were lucky in that the current production was the Oscar Wilde play *An Ideal Husband*, which had an elegant drawing room set complete with chandelier and a beautiful curving staircase for me to make my entrance. He started by chronicling 'the early years', reading a charming tribute that the president of the Royal Winnipeg Ballet Alumnus Association had sent over. He then announced me and I came down the staircase, feeling a bit like Norma Desmond in *Sunset Boulevard*. Gillian Lynne then appeared to make a speech about 'the middle years'. She was flattering and funny and recalled all the pictures and projects we'd done together. Andrew Leigh did 'the later years' about my years in management. He presented me with an inscribed silver salver; I cut the cake and made my response. It went well. I was on the verge of breaking down when recalling that Peg had been on that very stage in *Midsummer Night's Dream* all those years ago, but pulled myself together and finished strong.

Gillian and I walked off stage together to make our way round to front of house. She then chided me for retiring so young. 'You must do something to keep yourself occupied,' she said. 'I'm going to ring the Council for Dance, Education and Training. I know they're looking for inspectors.' Sure enough, the president of that organization, which is charged with monitoring the standards of the various dance schools and colleges, called the following week. She took me to lunch and persuaded me to become one of their associate inspectors. It sounded most appealing, going around the country, visiting the various colleges and keeping in touch with teaching trends. It did indeed prove fascinating, and rewarding. After all I had five years to get through before my pension would kick in. The Arts Council phoned. They had to keep track of the various companies they give money to, so would I attend any touring dance company in my area and write reports on the shows? Fine, this also got me out and about and kept my juices flowing. What I couldn't realise at the time, of course, was that this would prove to be the start of yet another career!

Adjustments had to be made on the home front. The idea was that I would sell the 'embassy', downsize to a more modest 'granny flat' and invest the profits to finance a modest income to tide me over till the pension started at sixty-five. I had one major problem. Henrietta! Don't laugh. Henrietta was a very elderly, much loved, longhaired tortoiseshell Persian cat and I felt that moving house at her age would be too distressing for her. Henrietta had arrived as a multi-coloured ball of fluff in 1981 when I was doing *Just a Verse and Chorus* at the Greenwich Theatre. She had outlived all her offspring and was now pushing seventeen. Despite all my friends' derision, she and I stayed on at that huge place until she finally went out into the garden, curled up under Peg's favourite white magnolia and quietly passed away.

I did then find a suitable retirement flat. This was another ground floor, but in a far more modest house and further away from the sea. The day I decided to buy, I paced it out. There were 603 paces down to the shore-edge. I felt I could cope. It was a one-bedroom but had a study where the thousands of Peg's books could live, plus a garage, although I'd given up driving as an unnecessary extravagance on retiring. I settled down, did my inspections for the CDET, reports for the Arts Council and life seemed nicely settled. Then I was headhunted!

Various organizations in the dance world, including the CDET, had been lobbying government for years to replace the rapidly disappearing local authority scholarships meant to help talented students through dance or stage schools. Formerly, if a student were offered a place at a major college, he would petition his local council and if his case was approved, draw on scholarship funds. With the shrinking of available resources and the wide disparity evident between one local authority and another, this was manifestly unfair. Finally, the government agreed to provide central funding for scholarships to the most talented students in the best schools around the country. The schools provide a range of three-year courses in dance, drama, stage management and musical theatre to sixteen-year-olds and over, leading to a professional qualifica-

The final curtain. My retirement speech at the Vic.

tion. The idea was not only to help fund the struggling student but also to raise the standards of the professional theatre.

The main proviso insisted on was that these courses and the colleges themselves would be validated and monitored by a totally independent body. Trinity College, London was chosen for this task. Trinity has been a respected examining body for 125 years. This was a slightly different task in that the college wouldn't be setting specific examinations but rather making judgements on the standards of training and student achievement across a varied range of courses. Unusually, it was agreed from the start that these decisions would not be made by academics, but by working professionals in their various fields. Accordingly, I was called up to London for interview and appointed Senior Assessor in Dance and Musical Theatre for the new scheme known as the National Dance and Drama Awards.

Here we go again! I was sixty-four.

Chapter 26

*Judging standards…the Dance and Drama Awards…the govern-
ment inspector…community learning provision…beside the sea…
leaving something behind*

First THINGS FIRST. It's no good pontificating on National Standards and trying to judge pass and fail levels unless you have seen what the technical and artistic standards actually are in the colleges around the country. There are three Senior Assessors in our section. We all have our own specialist areas, Dance and Musical Theatre for me, Classical Ballet for Brenda Garrett-Glassman and Contemporary Dance for Emilyn Claid. However, we all cross over to each other's areas for summative judgements. Accordingly, we set out to visit and make informal reports to Trinity College about each of the two dozen top schools in the initial scheme. These had been chosen because they were already receiving government funding from the Further Education budget and had been validated by the CDET inspections, some of which I'd just been involved in. Because Brenda and Emilyn are younger than I am (isn't everyone?) and still have busy careers in teaching and choreography to juggle, I ended up as the only person to visit all the schools around the country.

The new National Diplomas in Professional Dance/Classical Ballet/ Musical Theatre/Acting/Stage Management are three-year courses for sixteen-year-olds leading to a degree that will hopefully be transferable to other training if the dancer has an accident early in his career, for instance. The students have to reach high levels of professionalism in Preparation and Technique, Performance, Contextual Studies, Employment Skills and Health and Safety. The schools can devise their own individual courses and assessment methods, providing that they meet our criteria regarding artistic and technical ability and internally assess to level standards of fairness and equality across the board. Once approved for the scheme they are then able to offer tuition scholarships to their best students. We have a team of assessors who moderate the standards and progress of the students through their three years of study. A pilot scheme was put together to get it off the ground and the money quickly distributed to the students. The CDET had devised a set of criteria for the dance elements of the scheme and the equivalent organization in the drama world put together the acting and singing requirements. These sets of criteria, however, have proved over-elaborate and cumbersome in practice. I was therefore charged with devising new sets of criteria for the Dance and Musical Theatre Diplomas for the permanent scheme beginning in September 2004. Wow! More of this later.

After a year of working happily for Trinity College, I attended a meeting between OFSTED (the office for standards in education) and the course providers (the schools and colleges in the scheme). It developed that because of the money being allocated to the schools (£12,000,000 at that point) the government was insisting on each being subjected to a full official inspection by OFSTED to make sure the public was getting value for money. OFSTED needed specialist inspectors to carry this out. Aah! You're ahead of me. After reeling backwards clutching my brow on discovering the size of fees paid for this sort of work, I timidly applied. Sure enough, it was decided that I would go back to all the colleges I'd seen as a Trinity Assessor, but this time wearing another hat as an official government inspector. This was real grown-up stuff!

Instead of spending a day or so at a college, writing a fairly informal report and giving advice to them when wearing my Trinity College hat, I would now move in for the best part of a week with a Lead Inspector (a permanent Her Majesty's Inspector) who would write about the Leadership and Management of the institution while I, as Lead Curriculum Inspector, and a colleague would watch classes for three days and grade them on 'Achievements and Standards' and 'Quality of Education and Learning'. Each class would be graded individually and the institution would be given a final overall grade in both areas, one, how it was led and managed and two, how well the students were being taught and what standards they were attaining. We would then write the report, print it out and present it along with the agreed grades to the luckless principal on the Thursday. The principal reads it through for accuracy but is not allowed to challenge our decisions (except on formal appeal). The grade given to the school then determines whether it continues to receive funding. Believe me, it is not easy to tell a principal that you've known for several years that, despite all his or her hard work, the standards of achievement are still not satisfactory. You can suddenly see their future draining away before their eyes. It's a miserable situation for all concerned. If the standards of the profession are going to be improved, however, tough decisions have to be made. Fortunately, this happens very rarely and there's nothing more satisfying than the thrill of giving someone some extremely good news.

After a year of dashing around doing the Ofsted reports, combined with pre-validation visits to schools wanting to join the scheme, some as illustrious as the Royal Ballet Upper School and Ballet Rambert, I had a call from yet another inspectorate. This was the ALI (the Adult Learning Inspectorate). They are responsible for inspecting education for over-eighteen year olds. I agreed to inspect a wonderful drama school in central London for them. Although part of the same scheme, acting school intakes are eighteen plus as opposed to the dance-based schools for sixteen plus. Having survived the drama school, it was then decided I could do Adult Community Learning as well and I was sent down to Somerset to see what the local government authority was providing in the way of adult education. I found myself inspecting everything from Salsa classes for the over sixties to the Village Ladies' Choir. I suddenly seemed to have become the Dance, Drama and Singing guru to the nation from cradle to grave! It's now coming up to seven years since my abortive attempt at retirement and I'm busier than ever. Before going back to my most exciting activity, the setting of the National Criteria, I'd better update the state of house and home.

By pure chance, at the time I bought the modest retirement flat, the housing market in Brighton and Hove was about to go crazy. London was getting more and more impossible to live in with almost permanent semi-gridlock, and the coast, with its clean air and lovely Regency architecture, seemed more and more attractive. London is commutable in under an hour by train and Brighton has always attracted a lively and energetic, if rather louche, population. It has always had a large theatrical contingent commuting to the West End. To add to its many attractions, every few years or so large towns around the country vie to acquire official city status as it attracts business interests to the place. In the Jubilee year the Queen, in her wisdom, decided to bestow the honour on Brighton and Hove. Suddenly this became the place to live. I was perfectly happy in my little flat, but about then my upstairs neighbour decided to sell hers. When she told me her asking price, I was absolutely staggered. I decided, more or less as a joke, to put mine on the market for the same outrageous sum. The second couple through the door said, 'Fine, we'll take it'. In four years my humble little home had TREBLED in value!! I could hardly then refuse to sell, joke or no joke, so I set out to find somewhere else to live, pronto.

I don't know why I have this passion for living by the sea. Maybe it comes from being brought up on the prairies right in the middle of a continent. The concept of waking up each morning and looking out to sea, as I do now, seemed then to be an incredibly romantic and unlikely idea. I still find it exciting to pull back the curtains and check on whether the sea is flat and calm or whether the waves are crashing in. Mind you, this is living by the sea English fashion, very genteel and controlled, not rugged and wild.

When the then Prince Regent first made Brighton, and indeed the whole notion of coming down to the seaside, fashionable in the early nineteenth century, he built the extraordinary Brighton Pavilion as his palace by the sea. It remains as far over the top as it ever was and it's one's duty to shepherd gob-smacked visitors round it. The palace, and the fact that the nude beach is so casually part of the mainstream of Brighton life, are probably the two most astonishing facts of life to the average North American tourist. While Prinny was letting himself go with Indian and Asian extravagances, the Georgian/Regency architects were erecting some of the most beautifully elegant squares and terraces ever built for his wealthy burghers. Brunswick Square was one of the first examples in Hove, the quieter end of Brighton. Finished in 1850, the beautiful square on the seafront spreads its terraces along the front and I found myself another ground floor flat in one of these. The buildings are Grade 1 Listed which means they can never be changed, nothing can ever be built to impede their view, even the colour they must be painted is laid down in an Act of Parliament.

Doing so well on the first try at a retirement flat meant I could buy this one outright and not have a mortgage to worry about. I love it. I sit at my table by the window in the drawing room in the morning idly keeping one eye on the television (I'm a news junkie) and the other eye looking out to sea. Mind you, I've caught myself a couple of times wondering why the channel wouldn't change when I flicked the remote, till I realised I was pointing it at the window instead of at the telly. Ah, senility, where is thy sting?

The trouble is, I never seem to be here often enough. I've just come back from an eight-day inspection for the ALI of the Council provision of Adult Education in a large London suburb. I'm tired and think I should pull back a little. I am supposed to be retired after all. The one thing I am determined to push through, however, is the new sets of criteria for the Dance and Drama scheme. They soon go before the QCA, the authority in charge of approving the quality of curricula, and all looks well thus far, knock wood. If formally approved, the qualities of technique and artistry required for West End performers, for ballet and dance companies here and around the world will, in some small way, be set by me.

I think that's something to leave behind after all these years, don't you?

Chapter 27

ONCE UPON A TIME, a very long time ago, Gweneth Lloyd choreographed a ballet for the Winnipeg Company called *Wise Virgins.* The corps of wise and foolish virgins swirled and ran barefoot in choreography influenced by Gweneth's Greek dance background. The leading couple, dancing in a more classical style with the woman en pointe, were the Spiritual Apotheosis. The original male lead was Arnold Spohr, our erstwhile wedding witness, who later took over the artistic direction of the company. In 1955 the ballet was revived, renamed *Parable* and I took over the role. Danced to a glorious arrangement of Bach, it was a popular stand-by in both incarnations.

Thirty-odd years later a Dance academic in Toronto called Anna Blewchamp attempted to recreate the work with her students for her Master's degree. She went to Winnipeg to play the music to the original corps de ballet ladies, to stir their muscle memory, then arranged for my partner, Charlotte Wright, and me to meet and try to remember the leading roles. Luckily the project coincided with Ed Mirvish inviting the Old Vic management over to Toronto for the opening of his beautiful new theatre. Charlotte and I got together over there for the first time in three decades and surrendered ourselves to Bach as interpreted by Gweneth. Anna sent me a video of the finished recreation. It was fascinating stuff, although it's not entirely clear how close it came to the original.

The point of this anecdote, I suppose, is that I've reread the preceding chapters and think they need some sort of apotheosis. We're up to date and everything seems covered, but it seems to end with a bump. Perhaps I'm just finding it difficult to let go, but whatever the reason, here are a few more thoughts on what has been an eventful life, if nothing else.

First of all, memory. Everything that I remember, I remember in total and vivid detail. If I tell an anecdote, it is precisely as I recall it. The curious thing is that what I don't remember, I don't remember at all. There are sections of my life that aren't just hazy, they have disappeared entirely. I was going through some ancient BBC TV contracts a while ago and came upon a special I apparently did with Tennessee Ernie Ford. There was the contract, there was the payment advice, but I would swear on oath that I've never met the man. Weird!

Have I left things out? Well, yes. I took a conscious decision not to sensationalize, not to reveal where all the bodies are buried, and only take pot shots at those who thoroughly deserved it.

So what now? I think it really is time I slowed down a bit. The problem is, though, that although I'm perfectly content in my apartment by the sea and love pottering around and trying out new recipes and walking along the front, I still hate living by myself. It's nearly thirteen years since Peg died and I still haven't really come to terms with it. The bottom line is that I'll probably go on accepting work as long as they want me, just to keep occupied. I do have some loyal and loving friends down here. The day after Peg died, I suddenly realised that I could go out on my own for the first time in years without worrying about someone being there. It felt very strange. I left the flat and walked along the promenade. Coming towards me was a familiar figure. It turned out to be a chap called Nigel Mason, whom I had hired to work at the Vic back in 1983. He had qualified as a barrister, then turned to teaching and was now about to become a High Anglican priest. We had lost contact for ages and neither of us knew the other was living on the coast, so this chance meeting was an extraordinary coincidence. Through Nigel I met a diverse circle of people, mostly through his connections with the church. I tend to be the token heathen of the group, but no one seems to mind.

Do I mind getting old? Not really, but I do resent the physical changes. I know it's an old cliché seeing an old geezer reflected in a window and realizing with horror it's oneself, but it happens. Inside this old, fat, bald bloke in glasses is the slim, limber dancer I once was. One midsummer day a few years ago, I'd had a super day on the beach. The weather was perfect. I'd packed smoked salmon sandwiches and a cold bottle of wine for a treat at lunchtime. I'd swum several times and was now making my way home in the late afternoon feeling just fine. I was striding along, feeling all tanned and healthy, looking the world in the eye and feeling about twenty-five.

As I passed the crowded tables of an el fresco bar, however, a familiar voice called out 'Grandad, Grandad!' For a second I was tempted to ignore the call and the curious turned heads and carry on in my fantasy. However, I sighed, gritted my teeth, aged thirty years or so in an instant and joined my grandson, Trant, and his friends as they sat with their drinks in the sun. They were the real age that I had been feeling. I was back to being the old codger.

Still, I have my memories, and I treasure them. I'm glad I finally got some of them down on paper. When I start to forget them, I'll be able to get this out and remind myself that, despite all appearances, I was once a dancer.

Index